I Swear

I Swear

Politics Is Messier Than My Minivan

Katie Porter

CROWN
NEW YORK

Published in the United States by Crown, an imprint of Random House,
a division of Penguin Random House LLC, New York.

CROWN and the Crown colophon are registered trademarks of
Penguin Random House LLC.

LIBRARY OF CONGRESS CATALOGING-IN-PUBLICATION DATA
Names: Porter, Katie, author.
Title: I swear / Katie Porter.
Description: First edition. | New York: Crown, 2023.
Identifiers: LCCN 2022052257 (print) | LCCN 2022052258 (ebook) |
ISBN 9780593443989 (hardcover) | ISBN 9780593443996 (ebook)
Subjects: LCSH: Porter, Katie, 1974- | Political culture—United States. |
United States—Politics and government—2017-2021. | United States—
Politics and government—2021- | United States. Congress. House—
Biography. | Women legislators—United States—Biography. |
Women legislators—California—Biography.
Classification: LCC E901.1.P67 A3 2023 (print) |
LCC E901.1.P67 (ebook) | DDC 328.73/092—dc23/eng/20221207
LC record available at https://lccn.loc.gov/2022052257
LC ebook record available at https://lccn.loc.gov/2022052258

Printed in the United States of America on acid-free paper

crownpublishing.com

2 4 6 8 9 7 5 3 1

FIRST EDITION

Book design by Ralph Fowler

For my staff and volunteers.
You often stand behind me,
but you're leading the way to
a better America.

Contents

I Swear

1.

Not on the Ballot

I thought the hard part would be getting there.

My campaign for Congress began the night that Donald Trump won in 2016. And every day after that, I fought and worked to win. On a cold, blustery day in early January 2019, I was sworn in as the congresswoman for the 45th district of California.

After a two-year struggle, I'd made it to Congress. And yet, I continued to struggle just to show up for the job. I got lost in the byzantine tunnels of the Capitol that sent me in circles past industrial deep freezers and haphazard stacks of abandoned walnut furniture. I sat trapped on runways unable to physically fly to Washington. I arrived hot and sweaty, and always late, to press conferences, only to find myself straining on my tiptoes to be visible as men crowded in front of me.

On an overcast December morning, not quite one year into my first term, I managed to arrive at the correct location, on time, and draped in respectable fake pearls. In between residential townhouses just east of the Supreme Court, the empty French bistro was the kind of place that women gather for long, chatty lunches about their ski vacations and personal trainers. Normally closed to business at the early hour, it was open privately for one of the most powerful women in politics.

Stephanie Schriock, the president of EMILY's List, had arrived early too. After working directly on campaigns for years, Stephanie turned to mentoring hundreds of pro-choice Democratic women running for office. She smiled brightly and sat down across from me. The table was set for six, with four other recently elected congresswomen coming to the breakfast to join us. Stephanie ordered coffee and asked how I was doing as my first year in Congress neared its end and I geared up for reelection in the coming November.

"I am not on the ballot," I told her. She nodded mindlessly as she reached for a croissant. Then, realizing what I had said, she froze with her hand midair.

"What. Do. You. Mean?" she asked. Big Sister Stephanie, the cheerful mentor, was gone, replaced with Campaign Operative Schriock, hardcore party boss.

As the leader of EMILY's List, Stephanie was a salesperson, championing the need to elect more women, and her optimism and encouragement in the face of those challenges were legendary. But at this moment, she reverted to her former self, a warrior whose sole mission was winning elections for Democrats.

Her eyes locked on mine, and she repeated herself. "What do you mean, 'not on the ballot'?"

I took a deep breath and burst into tears. I told her that my staffer's plan to have me sign the declaration of candidacy in the presence of a notary in Washington, D.C., would not suffice to qualify me for the California ballot. The deadline was tomorrow, I was 2,670 miles away from the Orange County Registrar of Voters, and I needed to file in person. I would not be a candidate for reelection in 2020 unless I got there in the next twenty-seven hours. But what I didn't say was that the administrative mistake my staffer made with the ballot deadline felt like a divine sign that I did not belong in Congress.

Stephanie peppered me with logistical questions: What time was my flight to California? Were there any alternative flights if I missed my connection? How did this happen? Why didn't this get taken care of earlier? Whose fault is this? Never mind, we'll figure that out later.

"You can do this. You can still make it," she said, her peppy demeanor returning.

"No!" I said, swiping at my tears. "I don't want to! It's just too hard!" Writing this, I realize I sounded like a toddler. But I felt like a toddler, powerless against forces that were stronger than me, and out of solutions except rage.

Stephanie reminded me how hard I'd worked to get there and told me I couldn't give up now that I had finally won. Reelection every two years is just part of the process, she counseled. She told me that I was doing a great job and recounted a few stories of my success in congressional hearings, holding powerful men to account. I appreciated the flattery, but I was not having it.

I told Stephanie that I didn't care if I was good at being in Congress. I did not want to "find a way" or "juggle" or "get creative." I was so tired that I couldn't see straight. I didn't want to hear that I'd "laugh about it later" or that "maybe yoga" would help me relax, or any of the other cold comforts that get offered to working moms on the brink of ugly choices.

I escalated my voice, as much as appropriate, given our fine dining surroundings. "Listen to me: I'm beyond exhausted, my kids are suffering and angry, Congress is frustrating and broken, and I don't fit in here. I cannot do it."

During my first year in Congress, people had asked me almost every day, "How do you do it?" While I successfully deflected with phrases like "Don't look behind the curtain," and proffered platitudes like "One day at a time," I screamed on the inside. I was angry with Congress as an institution, and I was angry at myself for signing up to work in a system built for the benefit of old, rich, white men. While my colleagues marveled at sitting in the same chamber as our Founding Fathers, I was seething that those men had not only had wives but servants, or even slaves, to do their bidding while they endlessly debated in Washington, without any worry about their children getting to bed on time or doing their homework.

"But you can do it, Katie," Stephanie countered.

I then asked Stephanie the question I had asked myself every day for that year: "Oh yeah, then why am I the only single mother of young kids to serve in Congress?"

But I didn't give her the chance to answer. I knew why and I had finally said it out loud: It was just too hard.

When Congresswoman Donna Shalala arrived, she was oblivious to the tension in the room as Stephanie and I stared each other down. Donna, always happy to talk about herself and her accomplishments, diverted Stephanie. I retreated to eating my breakfast, having gotten the last word.

Sharice Davids and Susan Wild, also newly elected freshmen, arrived next, giving me sympathetic looks when they saw my puffy red eyes and smudged mascara. Both had their own challenges and hardships that year, but they seemed to me to be hanging on, if not bustling around importantly like Donna.

At the end of the meal, Stephanie held me back as the others departed. She was pointed: "Will you promise to fly to California this afternoon?"

I agreed to get on the plane, departing in just five hours, after I attended a hearing. But I still had an off-ramp. Stephanie had made me promise to travel to California, not to sign the candidate paperwork for reelection. The ballot fiasco felt like a confirmation that what I felt most days was true—being a single mom of young kids in Congress was not possible. Something had to give, and now I had failed at the most basic task of a politician: to run for reelection.

• • •

The first warning that Congress and my life were at odds was literally an alarm. My phone beeped, alerting me that a vote was taking place in the House of Representatives and counting down the fifteen minutes I had to make my way to the U.S. Capitol to be my community's representative in Washington.

That same January morning, I was sworn in on the House floor

On swearing-in day, I managed to get the kids into
dress clothes and not let them get run over.

and then voted to elect the Speaker of the House. After, I departed the Capitol to celebrate. Not only was this my first day as a congressperson, but January 3, 2019, was also my forty-fifth birthday. People had traveled to celebrate both occasions, and we rented a room and ordered a cake. I could not wait to hug my family, enjoy the moment with campaign staff, and catch up with old friends.

I was filled with relief as I entered the party. I was ready to take off my heels, have a piece of birthday cake, and relax away from the Capitol, where the expectation of being a "member" was heavy. I found my children devouring snacks, and I started to give hugs and shake hands. It was one of the best moments of my life—while it lasted.

We sang "Happy Birthday," and I cut slices of cake for guests, who ranged from my six-year-old daughter in her red velour dress to an octogenarian who gave me my first job out of college. I picked up a fork to have a bite of cake when my scheduler tapped my arm.

"Gotta go, ma'am," she said, pointing to the countdown for voting on her phone. I had been celebrating for fewer than twenty minutes when the majority leader had sudden aspirations to try to end the government shutdown that began a few days ago. Keeping the government open was obviously a necessary first step to all the wonderful policymaking aspirations that motivated my run for Congress. Still, I looked wistfully at the cake and then back at the clock ticking down.

"You can bring a slice of cake with you, ma'am," my scheduler said. "We gotta go."

I climbed into a car and headed back to the Capitol, clutching a smushed piece of birthday cake in a napkin. I felt that I truly embodied democracy in action as I rushed to the House floor and voted. Our government could start operating; federal workers could get paychecks. I turned to leave.

"Miss Porter, we have additional votes," said a floor staffer, whose entire profession is to get members to do their jobs by showing up to vote.

"On what?" I asked. I could take another quick vote to save our country, I thought, and still catch the end of the party and take my kids back to the hotel.

"Not sure yet. We don't have a compromise with the Republicans, so we have to keep trying things," she explained, and went to stop other congressmembers from leaving.

The session dragged on into the night. Hours passed as I voted on a "Motion to refer the resolution to a select committee with instructions to report it forthwith back" and other things that were gibberish to me. I started to worry. Who was watching my kids? Were they still awake? Were they wrestling in the hotel room, or worse, eating items from the hotel minibar? In the time-honored tradition of nagging mothers, my mom texted, "When will you be home?" My oldest son accusatorily messaged, "You said you would be right back, and it has been a LONG TIME." The best response that I could muster was that I was doing my best.

I asked a few colleagues and floor staff how long we would be, and everybody gave the same vague answers: Ideally soon, probably not past midnight, unclear but seems to be moving along. I made it back to the hotel five hours and eight votes later, but by then the birthday party had long ago ended. While the minibar looked intact, one child was missing. My legs ached, my dress had a frosting stain, and I could barely stand. I changed into leggings to go look for the missing child, reminding myself that he usually turned up eventually. I found him in the lobby, hustled the kids into pajamas, and climbed into bed, wanting to sleep but realizing that I needed to worry.

As a working parent, I consider scheduling my paramount skill. Time is the essence of life, and with enough colored markers and desk-sized calendars and chiming reminders, I can figure out how to meet work deadlines and make it to my kids' swim lessons. But my first day in Congress had gone off schedule—not by fifteen minutes or even thirty, but by hours and hours. Who could run their lives that way?

I had a sinking feeling as I indignantly posed that question to myself. I was new to Congress, but I had more than a decade of experience as a working parent. I knew the answer.

Men could. A man could live, perhaps thrive, in a system that requires walking out of the house on little notice, knowing someone else will remain behind, so he could tend to the ever-evolving responsibilities of his job. For a single mother like me, however, the absence of a schedule was a death knell.

Without the ability to plan, I couldn't find childcare. I couldn't tell my children not to worry, that I would see them later. I couldn't plan to use every minute wisely if I didn't know what needed to get done. I was doomed on day one.

• • •

Over the next year, I had days that stretched to the wee hours of the morning, and times that I was at home in California for fewer than twenty-four hours before I flew back across the country. I learned to dread the majority leader's updates. Was a "fluid situation" more or less certain than "Next vote: ??????" I scheduled, then canceled, then rescheduled parent-teacher conferences, visits to the pediatrician, scouting events, and birthday parties. I failed to wake up to get my kids off to school on time, and I left them unsupervised for the evening when I fell asleep at 6:00 P.M., badly jet-lagged. I would drag myself to the Capitol for 9:00 A.M. Democratic Caucus meetings that were at 6:00 A.M. California time, motivated only by the prospect of free bacon and a hope that there might be an announcement about the schedule.

I tried talking to House leadership and my congressional colleagues. The majority leader explained that they could not run Congress around my unique needs. Repeatedly, I heard that I had a "special situation." I came back with statistics about the 13.6 million other single parents in America. My family was not unusual. I tried pointing out the inefficiencies to taxpayers from wasted time and travel, and how endless disruptions prevented us from maximizing our time. I made a public (and unfavorable) comparison between the scheduling practices of the House of Representatives and my son's Cub Scout pack, which always planned its meetings a year in advance.

Sometimes people would suggest that I talk to someone else who had school-aged kids, but those were the most disheartening conversations of all. Male members told me that you just couldn't do this job without a partner, or that their spouses were essentially single parents. My fellow mothers talked about how hard it was even with their spouses helping at home. I felt that the implication was that I should find a husband. Nobody had answers, but my older female colleagues were the least helpful. Most had entered politics either after their children were in college or because a spouse or father had been elected. Nancy Pelosi followed both of these traditional paths into politics for women, even as her election as the first woman Speaker of the House was groundbreaking. Chastised for pushing for changes to make it possible for a single mother to serve in Congress, I was met again and again with the same sentiment: *What did you expect?*

In fact, I had carefully studied the House calendar before I ran for office. I tallied the number of days required in Washington, D.C., the longest stretch that I would be away from my children, and how the district work periods in my community could match up with my kids' school vacation schedules. I failed to have the insider knowledge, however, that the House "schedule" was not a way of marking fixed times and set patterns. Voting times and days were merely aspirational, and politicians can definitely be counted on to fall short of their aspirations.

• • •

As the ballot deadline loomed twenty-two hours away, I boarded my flight back to Orange County. I hoped, half-heartedly, for a delay on the tarmac. I calculated that if I missed my connection and had to drive halfway across the country, it was already too late. I wondered if a winter storm would again disrupt my travel, and I fantasized about being a professor again. I pushed down the guilt I felt in knowing that the district would likely be represented by a Republican if I did not run for reelection. When we did take off, I tried to sleep but continued to wrestle with what was the right choice: fight to stay in Congress or take care of my kids? Whose needs came first? Did my well-being even matter in this?

The next morning, I did what working mothers do every day. I put one foot in front of the other and tried to do it all. My best friend came to pick me up, bringing coffee and good cheer, and took me straight to the Registrar of Voters. I had made it physically there, even if I felt like an imposter. I wasn't sure how long I could survive the hardships, but the answer was clearly at least one more day.

I signed the paperwork, thankful that there were no questions on the forms about being a good mother or what this job took out of my kids. I also wasn't required to pledge to like the job or to make our political system functional. While it was a tough standard for some Republicans at that time, the oath only required me to support and defend the Constitution. That I could do. I raised my hand and said the magic words: *I swear.*

I was on the ballot.

• • •

The following morning, I again put one foot in front of the other, walking back down the jet bridge for a plane out of California. I didn't go back to Washington, D.C., though. I did what kids of all ages do when they need help: I went home.

Iowa's cornfields were dusted with snow when I arrived. My dad picked me up, offering a warm IOWA STATE sweatshirt in place of my tailored suit jacket, and drove me to his house. The next day, the political staffer assigned to shepherd me around Iowa fell victim to my stepmother's hospitality. The staffer's sole goal was to get me out of the house on time, and to manage it, she had to accept half a pan of cinnamon rolls and a thermos of coffee. With that, we headed to where I had grown up.

Creston, Iowa, was the Union County seat. Growing up on a farm twenty-five miles away, this was the big town where we went to the dentist or library. Its population was 7,536 in the last census. Several downtown storefronts were vacant, but we entered one covered with placards touting WARREN FOR PRESIDENT. This was one of dozens of field offices that Elizabeth Warren's campaign had opened in Iowa, in advance of its infamous caucus in February 2020.

I went to the front of the room and told the story of growing up in Iowa, watching land prices plummet and hearing of farmers losing their family's land to the bank. Gray heads in stocking caps nodded in shared memory. I shifted into advocating for Elizabeth Warren, whom I had endorsed a few weeks before, and then opened up the floor for questions.

A woman in the front row raised her hand. "Katie, it's good to see you again. You sound just the same." I squinted; who was this person? Mercifully, she continued, "I'm Mary Seales, I was your preschool teacher in Lorimor, Iowa, in the one-room preschool your mom helped start. You were always stubborn, and you would get frustrated but never give up. You keep giving them hell in Washington. We're real proud of you."

Over the next two days I shuttled around Iowa, from cozy corner coffee shops to basement recreation rooms. Everywhere, I campaigned for Warren, explaining her plans to protect and uplift hardworking Americans. I heard organizers and regular Iowans talk about the rigged system in Washington, a place where the rules were designed to keep power, not create opportunity. I found myself nodding along when people talked, and responding not by making excuses but by sharing experiences of my own that confirmed that our political system indeed needed to be better. I quit pretending that I loved it and instead laid bare all the ways Washington not only ran on a schedule that excluded ordinary people but also made policies that left ordinary people behind. As I talked, I felt my determination to continue in Congress bubble up above the exhaustion and frustration.

I hadn't found any relief in getting on the ballot for reelection. It was just another procedural hurdle, with unnecessary paperwork and a cross-country journey to comply with arcane rules, a bureaucratic nightmare that was an awful lot like my first months being in Congress. But in those two days in Iowa, I remembered that I did not go to Washington to learn how to play by the rules. I went to Washington to rewrite them. If Congress didn't work for me, I would keep trying. If I was bumped and bruised for the effort, and ultimately could not succeed, it was not for naught. As the first working single mother of young children to serve in Congress, I was a trailblazer. It was not about how far I made it or if I emerged from the trail unscathed. My work was to make space for others to follow, to create a wider path that welcomed different kinds of people to be bigger voices in our democracy. My journey in Congress was going to be a rough ride, but I was not going to turn around.

2.

Positive Campaign

Sometimes I accomplish things without even trying. Only rarely, but the effortless achievements are out there. And a good place to find out what I'm doing—intentionally and unintentionally—is social media. When I ran for Congress, I wanted to be an example of how women can "have it all" when it comes to career and family. I wanted to inspire my community to believe in government and to make serious policies that help families. On Twitter, I get positive feedback of hearts and likes and thumbs-up and comments that show that my hard work toward these goals is paying off.

But along with these superfans, I have the opposite. I call these users "superdumps" because they dump on anything I do. If I have been feeding the homeless, my sack lunches do not contain enough fiber. If I am at an outdoor tree-planting event, it looks like I forgot sunscreen. If I am at a pet adoption event, did I know that turtles do not like to be held that way? (No, I did not.) My sincere efforts are not good enough for some people, and as an elected official, I get to hear about it. Social media stirs up strong emotions, and so does politics. When they mix, it's potent.

It comes with the job, I tell myself. I cannot represent people if I do not know what they think: the policies they desire, their views on Congress, and their ideas for me. It takes tremendous effort, and a lot of scrolling through social media feeds, to take it all in, but the effort pays off.

But without any effort at all, I have managed to land right in the middle of one social media war: the one between fat-shamers and body positivity people. I certainly don't want to be in this fight, but apparently I'm remarkably successful at stimulating this policy debate.

Reading through the congratulatory messages on social media after I won in November, I saw: "One benefit of the 2018 election is people like Stacey Abrams and Katie Porter running fat-positive campaigns." I have to give it to this person. I had not, until that moment, appreciated my accomplishments as a fat person. In fact, I had not realized that I was officially fat, much less observed to be apparently feeling positive about it.

Shortly after gaining this insight, I burst into tears. I have been chubby, I have been heavy, and I have been a bigger person. But after three pregnancies and a couple of stints at Weight Watchers, I have also been average and healthy. Through it all, I made the choice to avoid scrutinizing my body. Plus, when you are a professor, which I had been for ten years before running for office, you have a podium that covers everything. That wooden box is handy for balancing the lecture notes and eliminating the need for shapewear at the same time.

In running for Congress, I had overlooked this aspect of public service—the need to be an example of physique. A lot of blood, sweat, and tears went into the rest of my campaign to become a leader, to be respected for my mind and my values. And now here I was serving not as a savvy public policymaker or exemplar of steely character, but as a fat-positive role model.

I continued reading the social media post—but soon wished I

hadn't. The comments that followed this initial observer's ebullience described the harms of obesity and the cost of overweight people on our healthcare system. Others countered by noting the psychological harms of fat-shaming. People argued that if I could not control my appetite, how could I control the national deficit? My supporters noted that the Republican I had beaten was skinny, so voters clearly preferred me. Others observed that Trump was fatter. (This did not have the effect of cheering me up.)

• • •

Growing up, I was always a little round. There were warnings from the pediatrician and a definite preference for elastic-waist shorts. When uniforms were distributed for middle school volleyball, I made sure to dive in to get a larger size, but there was always one to fit me. I never felt fat; I just felt on the cusp of it, as if any day I could cross that threshold.

Of course, ideas about body image are different in Iowa. When you make a casserole, you can use a normal 9"x13" pan, or you can upgrade it to feed half the town. My brother calls this "funeral size," because it's suitable for an entire church basement gathering of the bereaved.

The recipes reflect that culture and the corresponding body sizes. In our family cookbook, the Norwegian meatball recipe starts with five pounds of ground beef, which translates to three hundred hand-formed meatballs. Other markers of a funeral-sized Midwestern recipe include anything that takes more than one box of Jell-O or that uses an entire bottle of salad dressing. Even when the portions are scaled down, the ingredients can get out of whack. Many an Iowa recipe calls for bacon as an ingredient in more than one part of the dish (e.g., Bacon-Wrapped Jalapeño Poppers, stuffed with cream cheese and, you guessed it, bacon).

This meant that I was never the fat kid in my class in Iowa. That distinction belonged to the school bully, Johnny Jo Holtry. Yep, that is his real name, and I'm pretty sure he would never vote for a Democrat anyway. I wasn't even the largest girl. With a school cafeteria that featured "chicken-fried chicken," several of my classmates were well padded enough to survive the cold weather and hard knocks of rural life. And while Iowa is not to be confused with Idaho, Iowans do eat a lot of potatoes. My mother's signature dish is something called Country Club Potatoes, which involves an entire stick of butter and tastes great for breakfast, lunch, or dinner.

Notwithstanding her recipes, my mom made efforts to police my weight. She was always thin, perhaps as a consequence of chain-smoking, but who am I as a chubby daughter to comment on her vice? She did her duty, warning me to watch my night snacking and cautioning that I didn't want to have to start donning the dreaded "husky girls" clothing. In retrospect, I am pretty sure that those velour turtlenecks and corduroy pants don't look good in any size.

• • •

Campaign T-shirts are similarly unattractive, partly because they generally come in the same unisex shape—also known as no shape at all. On top of that, they shrink, wrinkle, and are not necessarily made from natural fibers. I fear some of the early Katie Porter merchandise was no better, but I did advocate for a flattering V-neck. An underrated aspect of the growing number of women in elected office is that more political T-shirts now come in a women's cut. As of this writing, I'm not quite enough of a public figure to be able to offer that variety of merch, but maybe this book will put me over the top. Go to www.katieporter.com/shop and leave comments about the need for flattering styles, and maybe my campaign manager will cave.

When the Katie Porter T-shirts went live for sale, the first thing we ran out of was 3XLs. Then 2XLs, then XLs, and right down the line until we hit smalls. The original order of smalls is not sold out, even two years later. Maybe this is because my large-and-in-charge persona (and body size) attracts a, shall we say, "larger" fan base. Or maybe, in a political world of big personalities, nobody wants to be small, even in T-shirts.

Politicians themselves, though, are a thin group. Indeed, this was one of President Obama's most praised qualities, and a frequent point of comparison with Donald Trump. During my campaign and time in office, as I went from a size 12 to a 14 to a 14W to my current 16W, I reverted to my childhood defense—at least I wasn't the largest person in my class, the new congressmembers elected in 2018.

Or wait—maybe I was. My class featured miniature men like Max Rose and wispy women like Mary Gay Scanlon, but nobody on the other side of the scale. (That is a pun.) Some were incredibly fit, like former NFL player Colin Allred, or tall and rail thin, like Lori Trahan. In what was widely described as the most diverse class ever elected to Congress, I was not just the only single mom of young kids, I was also the class fatty.

But it took social media to give me the epiphany that I held that title. And I guess I'm grateful for that new understanding. In a world of supposed identity politics, I get to have an extra mantle. In addition to elevating issues like childcare, I could take on this avatar of fat success.

But I'm not going to. I don't plan to become thin anytime soon, although thinner does seem within grasp when I have fewer kids and constituents to put ahead of diet and exercise. And it's not that I'm opposed to thin. In a later online debate about my fatness, someone commented, "Katie Porter knows she needs to work on her weight but she is actually a lovely person." Um, thanks?

The reason that I rage about such Twitter posts is that I fail to see how my weight connects to my work. To be a congressperson, you need to be thoughtful and courageous and creative and smart. You do not need to be thin. Being in shape helps, because politicians do a great deal of running around, back and forth, to hearings and meetings and votes and receptions featuring calorie-bomb hors d'oeuvres. I take an average of 15,000 steps each day that I am on Capitol Hill, tackling the big marble staircases to get to the House Chamber to vote. In fact, in a contest at the House gym, I did four times the number of push-ups that Congresswoman Abigail Spanberger did. That is badass, given that she was a CIA operative before she ran for Congress. At least until you consider the actual number of push-ups (one!) performed by Abigail, which just makes us both look bad.

The real question is, Why is one's size a political issue? Why do we vote for tall, thin people and not short, chubby people? There is an argument about self-control that emerges periodically in my Twitter feed that goes something like this: *How can we trust her to vote correctly on taxes if she doesn't have the self-control to avoid cupcakes?* Even if you buy that line of thinking, I assure you there are plenty of politicians for whom self-control is a struggle. For example, Matt Gaetz, the congressman from Florida, lacks the control to think before he speaks. Ted Yoho clearly lacked self-control when he decided to yell at Alexandria Ocasio-Cortez on the steps of the Capitol. These gentlemen may be thin, but they definitely have questionable judgment.

Politicians make plenty of poor choices, but the empirical data on self-control points to judgment problems, such as committing felonies, that run deeper than food choices. Maybe the real lapse in decision-making is daring to run for office as a larger person; it's a choice that inevitably seems to bring the consequence of body shaming. In America's two-party system, being an elected official already means roughly half the population disagrees with you about most things. The real sin isn't gluttony; it's hubris in thinking you can get away with being both wrong and fat.

Of course, weight isn't the only way we judge the appearance of our elected officials. Adam Schiff probably went through life never thinking about his neck before he stood up for our democracy and was labeled "Pencil Neck." Mitch McConnell might have liked turtles before those memes started circulating. Maybe even Donald Trump's little hands weren't an issue when he wasn't waving them in our faces.

Our elected officials let us down in all sorts of ways, from being disengaged to letting privilege distort their understanding of our needs. The fact that all politicians are not attractive or at an ideal weight is the least of the problems with our democracy. My advice

A great action shot of me visiting the U.S.-Mexico border, where I look professional and proportional. This photo never made it off my staffer's camera roll. SAD!

A terrible action shot of me visiting the U.S.-Mexico border, where my stomach protrudes so I look pregnant. This photo was posted to my 1.1 million Twitter followers. SAD!

is that in upcoming elections, if you face a choice between two excellent candidates who share your values, vote for the fat one. Or the ugly one. Or the short one. Or the bald one. These folks will stay humble because social media will keep them that way.

And that will make for a stronger democracy, for representatives who do not forget that they are one election away from being just another American. Plus, there is a direct benefit for you. The more we debate body positivity in elected officials, the less anyone will look too carefully at just how many cookies you needed to survive Trump's presidency.

3.

Mistakes

The phone started ringing at 4:00 A.M. I was totally disoriented fielding the first few calls, mumbling that they should dial me at work. Eventually, I was alert enough to ask a caller, who identified himself as working at a radio station with a lot of *K*s and *X*s in its name, why people were calling me for interviews at the crack of dawn.

"We read the article, of course," he said.

"Um, what article?"

"Lady, you are on the front page of *The New York Times*. Don't you get the paper?"

In fact, I did not get that paper delivered to my door in Coralville, Iowa. As I learned later that day when I went to buy a copy, there was only one place in town that even sold *The New York Times*.

The University of Iowa College of Law, where I was a junior professor, lacks the media reach of places like New York University or Harvard Law. How did these media folks get my home number? Also, if the phone did not stop ringing, how was I going to get my toddler, Luke, through his morning routine of the Elmo *Wild Wild West* video and bundled off to day care in time to teach my classes?

I didn't have much time to worry about either. On that morning,

November 6, 2007, radio stations all over the East Coast wanted me to be their morning guest, newspapers wanted quotes, and TV bookers were continually asking if I had a preferred local studio. I had just published a paper about mortgage companies and home-owners who failed to pay. After three years of research, I was excited somebody wanted to hear about property law more than my students did. Now fully awake, I eagerly said "yes" to every press request.

The project began in 2004. As the real-estate economy boomed, the homeownership rate soared, and Wall Street ratcheted up sales of mortgage-backed securities. Meanwhile, I looked in the other direction: down. Bankruptcies happen even in good economic circumstances, and building on research that I started at Harvard, I was studying the families on the losing end of homeownership and experiencing foreclosure.

Relatively ahead for those times, I had a pink BlackBerry that I had purchased to read my email while I looked after my son. The research had grown in the first two years of his life, even if taking care of him was all I felt like I'd done on many days. That morning, as he ate Cheerios in his high chair, I scrolled through congratulatory messages in the little window of my BlackBerry.

Several people forwarded the *New York Times* article "Dubious Fees Hit Borrowers in Foreclosures," and one sent a picture of the hard copy. Right at the top, above the fold, business reporter Gretchen Morgenson had written about my study. I had circulated a draft version of my research to a handful of consumer lawyers for their feedback. One of them sent it along to Gretchen. I hadn't spoken to her, but she had clearly read my paper. The article described the widespread questionable or illegal practices of mortgage companies my research had documented. My study also showed that families were getting cheated even in bankruptcy, a system designed to help them save their homes.

At that moment in November, the economy was still humming along. Earlier in 2007, the chairman of the Federal Reserve, Ben Bernanke, had told Congress that "despite ongoing adjustments in the housing sector, overall economic prospects for households remain good. Household finances appear generally solid, and delinquency rates on most types of consumer loans and residential mortgages remain low." The takeaway from his economic jargon was that families could trust Wall Street and Washington, D.C., that our economy would be fine. But while unemployment was low and consumer spending continued upward, the number of people in bankruptcy also hit an all-time high. A handful of consumer advocates, including me, were pointing to major problems in the economy. Almost nobody listened.

• • •

"The Debtor is an 83-year-old woman with minimal schooling and limited financial resources. Fairbanks is a corporation organized and existing under the laws of Utah." Given that opening to the court's recitation of the facts of the case, the odds looked grim for Pearl Maxwell, a senior citizen fighting to keep her home. The bankruptcy judge was ruling in Pearl's bankruptcy on whether her mortgage company could foreclose on her house. The property, at 49 Stockton Street in Dorchester, Massachusetts, was built nearly a hundred years before. A chain-link fence and a couple of cement steps separated the porch from the street. Pearl had owned the house for twenty-four years, living now with her granddaughter.

On a raw spring day in 1988, a door-to-door construction salesman climbed onto the porch and proposed repairs to Pearl's home. New siding and windows with no money down, and the salesman had an arrangement with a lender who would make the deal. Pearl signed a loan and refinanced not even three years later for an even higher amount. In 1991, she owed $149,150.50. The accuracy of that accounting was the last time everyone agreed on what Pearl owed.

Over the next decade, one lender after another collected payments from Pearl and sold the loan on to a new entity in the red-hot mortgage securities market. Rinse and repeat a few times, and ten years later, in 1999, Pearl owed money to a company she'd never heard of. And she owed a *lot* of money, more than she had even borrowed, due to the ballooning payments and pyramiding fees. Facing a foreclosure sale and living only on Social Security, she filed bankruptcy the day before she was supposed to lose her home. In response, Fairbanks, the lender, made an internal note in its system: "Customer filed bankruptcy. This is a stall tactic because I doubt she can afford to cure our delinquent amount. . . . We'll see her back on f/c [foreclosure] soon."

As the world would learn a decade later, in 2009, when millions of loans like Pearl's became delinquent and foreclosures spiked, mortgage companies were not very good at making predictions. With home prices rising and the economy expanding, many lenders and borrowers believed that only a real deadbeat could get into financial trouble. The dominant mindset was that "the bank is always right" and could be trusted to give you a good deal on a loan.

The young lawyer, Tara Twomey, who represented Pearl asked Fairbanks for documents to back up its effort to take Pearl's home. Fresh out of law school, Tara simply followed the law as written, and the rule was perfectly clear. In bankruptcy, a creditor seeking to get paid needed to attach a copy of the promissory note (the loan), a copy of the mortgage (the document that gives the lender the right to take the property if not paid), and a detailed itemization of the amount owed.

Fairbanks was sure of the interest rate: 16%. It was very sure that Pearl could not pay and that it could take her home. Fairbanks struggled with every other point. Without any paperwork in its own systems, Fairbanks tried to get Pearl to give it a copy of any documents she had. Undeterred by its shoddy records, Fairbanks sent debt collection letters demanding various amounts. On April 16, 1999, the bank told Pearl she owed $264,603—nearly double the amount she had borrowed ten years earlier. Even worse, just a week later, Pearl got a letter saying she owed $363,603, a cool $99,000 more.

Fairbanks argued that it didn't matter whether the company followed the law because Pearl was "unable to remember or understand numerous documents" and that "there are no damages since . . . she did not understand any credit terms." The bank's argument boiled down to blaming Pearl for being uneducated and old, precisely why she was targeted for the subprime loan in the first place. But Tara asked the judge to enforce the law. With no evidence to show how much Pearl owed or that it had the right to foreclose, the lender had no rights.

The judge agreed, calling the lender's arguments callous and appalling. She ruled the original loan was an unconscionable contract, wondering how the lender could expect repayment when the amount of the monthly mortgage payment was 98.5% of Pearl's and her granddaughter's combined incomes. Although Fairbanks blamed Pearl for not shopping for a better deal than the one that arrived at her front door, the judge let Pearl unwind the terrible loan. Through bankruptcy, Pearl was able to use the law to keep her home.

A legal aid lawyer committed to representing people in poverty, Tara was heady with the victory. An elderly low-income Black woman could stay in her home, beating a big corporation whose stock was soaring on Wall Street. Tara wondered at her luck that Fairbanks had just made mistake after mistake. Then she wondered if maybe it was not luck at all.

Maybe banks actually could not keep track of their own money?

Tara approached then professor Elizabeth Warren asking for her help in researching whether Pearl was a one-in-a-million borrower who could beat the bank, or whether millions of dollars in bank loans were badly documented. Warren was busy, but she told Tara that perhaps a newer scholar looking for a project would take an interest. In 2004, she introduced me to Tara in an email.

My childhood was a long lesson in the banks winning and borrowers losing. Pearl's story seemed like a fairy tale, with Tara as godmother, working some legal magic to prevent foreclosure. I was doubtful about doing research to see how often banks broke the law. If such a study was so promising, Warren would have done it herself. She had an army of Harvard students as research assistants (I had been one only a few years before). With a big budget and the platform at Harvard to reach policymakers, Warren was clearly better positioned to do this project. I was a baby professor and had five years to produce enough publications to earn tenure. With banks winning creditor-friendly changes to bankruptcy law in 2005, I could write paper after paper explaining the new laws. To publish successfully merely required me to read, think, and write.

To prove Tara correct, I would need to design a study, find funding, get human subject research approval, build a database, obtain thousands of pages of court files, code the results, conduct statistical analysis, and then, after all that, write a paper. The project was time-consuming and risky, and if we found nothing interesting, I could lose my professorship for failing to produce quality research. I have never been afraid of hard work, but I am also not stupid.

"Maybe," I told Tara, not wanting to disappoint her. "Let's keep talking."

Every few weeks, Tara would email. She wondered if I might have more time in the fall when I started my first law-teaching job at the University of Nevada, Las Vegas. She suggested an idea for research funding. She had law students working in her legal aid clinic who might be willing to help as research assistants. She cheered when I finished my first paper on rural bankruptcies, freeing me up for a next project.

The most dreaded question that a young professor gets asked is "What are you working on?" The truthful answer is almost always "Nothing" because your first few years of teaching are plenty hard enough. But you cannot say that, or your senior colleagues will question your productivity. So, Tara's idea for a study became my go-to answer. I am designing a whole new project to look at creditors' compliance with bankruptcy mortgage law, I would explain. "Good luck" was the inevitable response. Back then, I wasn't as skilled at making complex ideas simple—and I didn't carry a whiteboard around like I do now.

Having offered up the mortgage study enough times, however, meant that people were expecting progress. Hedging my bet by working double-time on an article about the new bankruptcy law, I got started with Tara by writing a grant proposal. Upon receiving funding, I had another set of demands for progress, and we moved forward with building a database and collecting thousands of pages of court files. Our sample was 1,700 bankruptcies of people trying to save their homes from foreclosure. In each case, we waded through the files. What did the homeowner say was owed? What was the bank trying to collect? Where was the paperwork?

More than half the time, banks failed to attach the required documents. Without the mortgage or loan paperwork, lenders still tried to collect. They added on the usual penalties, like late fees that totaled thousands, and ridiculous charges like "fax fees" of $50, overnight delivery for $137, and even $5,391 described only as "other."

Having continued to represent struggling homeowners, Tara was not surprised. Since Pearl, she had started asking for documentation in every case. She learned firsthand what the research study concluded: Mortgage companies were cheaters. But that was still breaking news in late 2007, when *The New York Times* published the results.

• • •

A week after those middle-of-the-night calls asking for interviews, I flew to Austin, Texas, to present my research. A couple hundred bankruptcy lawyers were gathered in a ballroom at the Four Seasons to rustle their sports pages and drink lukewarm coffee for the next eight hours to satisfy their requirement for continuing legal education. Much of the day consisted of panels of attorneys describing recent cases and the new bankruptcy laws, but I took the stage alone. Behind me, a huge screen showed graphs and figures of my findings.

In four out of ten cases, the mortgage company demanded that the judge order payment or foreclose on the home but failed to provide any evidence of the loan terms. Seventy percent of lenders tried to collect more money than the homeowner thought they owed. In our sample of 1,700 cases, banks asked people to pay a total of $6 million more than expected. In the entire system, across the country, hundreds of millions of dollars were being paid on shaky evidence. Yet nobody was doing anything about it. Debtors' attorneys rarely demanded the paperwork, and in virtually every case, attorneys, judges, and bankruptcy trustees—the supposed "watchdogs" of the system—ignored the rules. I finished my speech and was met with dead silence.

I waited a few more beats and scanned the ballroom. In my classroom, sometimes a reluctant student would speak up to break awkward silence. I eventually saw a hand in the back, an older gentleman in a suit that might have cost as much as Pearl's door-to-door loan. He stood up.

"Young lady," he said, "Wells Fargo does *not* make mistakes."

I blushed as he lectured me like a school principal on how Wells Fargo had many levels of executives, lawyers, and accountants. With more years of experience, he said, I would understand just how complicated this area of law was.

"Wells Fargo is one of the largest banks in the country," he went on. "We can certainly afford to follow the law."

Heads swiveled back to me on the stage.

"Of course, you have a point," I began conciliatorily, "but—"

I was cut off, as other lawyers piped up:

"I always follow the rules."

"Maybe the borrower was okay with paying whatever the bank said was owed."

"A lot of these homeowners owe more than the house is worth anyway."

I pointed out that the law did not vary depending on the circumstances. Banks had flaunted the rules to foreclose but were being allowed to do exactly that—even when they made clear mistakes.

Then came attacks on the integrity of my research.

"I don't see this in my cases, so I don't know where you got these files."

"How do we know you picked the cases at random?"

"You must have found a few bad apples."

The study was large, the sample was random, and the files were in the public record. These objections reflected the conventional wisdom of many decades: Banks are always right. We had over a thousand cases with serious flaws, and I was being rebuffed with an analogy to fruit.

The bad-apple objection was bassackwards, as my granddad would say. The original reference, and the scientific fact, is that one bad apple actually *does* spoil the whole barrel. I know this because many times I have returned from Washington to discover this miraculous microbial process at work in my produce drawer.

But even the correct metaphor was not apt. Tara and I had un-covered the fact that mortgage companies violated the law over half the time. The barrel itself was rotten, and everything that went in stood a high chance of rotting too.

I rebuffed critique after critique. Yes, of course we had done checks to make sure the data was coded correctly. No, the problem was not just Countrywide, the giant mortgage lender.

I stood my ground that day, having practiced a few months ear-lier. As part of my progress toward tenure, the University of Iowa's most eminent law professor, David Baldus, was asked to review my paper, "Misbehavior and Mistake in Bankruptcy Mortgage Claims." Baldus was my senior colleague and had done groundbreaking re-search to show racial disparities against Blacks in death penalty sentences.

His reaction to my paper was not favorable, and I feared that I had followed Tara's passionate advocacy into a dead end. Baldus particularly hated my title, saying it was reckless to characterize the bank's actions as "misbehavior and mistake," when all of them could have been mistakes. I had no evidence of intentional misbehavior, at least not the kind that is needed to be criminal. To appease Bal-dus, a member of my tenure committee, I had been weighing whether to change the paper's name to one of his suggestions: "Some Evidence of Inaccuracies in Mortgages" or "Preliminary Re-search on Mortgage Compliance."

That day in Texas, as criticism came from all corners of the ball-room, I decided to believe the banker in the back. He had pro-claimed that "Wells Fargo does not make mistakes," and that it had plenty of money to follow the law. The only alternative was that banks' repeated failures to obey the law were a deliberate strategy. Breaking the rules was cheaper and easier than following them, and for years nobody had gotten caught.

My research didn't send any bankers to jail, but people started to ask questions. Several months after the headlines, I was asked to testify before the obscure Senate Subcommittee on Administrative Oversight and the Courts. Senator Chuck Schumer brought out a poster board with a quote. The Countrywide Mortgage CEO had told Wall Street analysts about how foreclosure fees, late charges, and the like were "part of our diversification strategy, a counter-cyclical diversification strategy" to profit even when Countrywide was not making money on new loans. Senator Schumer was amazing at that hearing, and I thought that punishment would rain down on the lawbreaking banks.

At best, there was a drizzle. For nearly five more years, from 2007 until 2012, banks kept preying on homeowners in foreclosure and kept mocking laws intended to protect consumers. While I had started to change minds and get people in power to see that mortgage companies made mistakes and misbehaved, I did not want to be right. I wanted *things* to be right. Banks used the law to try to collect every penny; we should expect them to follow every rule.

Pearl kept her blue clapboard house in Dorchester, but four million Americans lost their homes. I had found a problem and I had gotten front-page publicity for it. What I hadn't done was anything to fix it. Professors did studies, not make policies.

Katie's Guide to Consumer Protection

Bring the receipts.
Plan for the scam by keeping paperwork and reading the fine print, especially about cancellations and refunds.

Phone a friend.
When I found a great apartment, Rep. Rashida Tlaib said, "Katie, that seems too good to be true." Sure enough, the alleged landlord was in prison. Get a second opinion.

Never feel ashamed.
They cheated YOU! They are the bad guys. Would you report a burglary? It's no different when a company rips you off. Expect them to make it right.

Be noisy.
File a written complaint, leave a review, or stop doing business with the bad guys. Even if you come up empty-handed, your action can warn others to watch out.

Stick it to the man.
Corporations count on us giving up. Despite the automated recording, your time and your call are <u>not</u> important to them. Persist.

Sorry isn't good enough.
Businesses apologize, dressing this up as exceptional customer service ("We're pleased to offer 10% of your money back"). Ask for the remedy you deserve.

Bring on the whiteboard.
Crooked companies can often beat individuals, but a government investigation and bad publicity can break them. Report the wrong to government.

4.

218

In the spring of 2019, I was dog-tired. My scheduler was filling every minute of every day, often forgetting to include time for lunch or dinner, which was harrowing for everyone as I get hangry. My round-trip commute between Orange County and Washington, D.C., was nineteen hours a week. Since I was sworn in a few months before, I hadn't spent more than ten consecutive days on either coast.

I collapsed on a bench on the House floor one evening during a series of votes. A freshman colleague from California walked past, looking chipper, energetic, and, frankly, a little bit smug. Maybe, I thought desperately, he would have advice on what I was doing wrong. "I just don't understand how you do it," I said to him. "The hearings, the votes, the meetings, the travel, the fundraising. It's exhausting."

He raised an eyebrow. "I think you and I have very different ideas about how to do this job," he said.

"What do you mean?" I asked.

"My job is to be Vote 217. Your job is to be Vote 218," he said pointedly, referring to the number of votes needed to pass a bill in the House. He gestured at the vote tally displayed overhead. "Vote with the Democrats. Get reelected. That is your job."

I'd thought that I was the voice of the people of California's 45th District in Washington, D.C. Apparently, that was equivalent to being cast as Tree #7 in the elementary school play. The right way to do the job was just to show up—get onstage and try not to trip. I was not there to excel or lead. My colleague's message was clear: I was doing it wrong. I had only myself to blame for being worn out and frustrated. My hard work in asking questions and trying to change policy was visible to my colleagues; they just thought it was a waste of time.

· · ·

In February 2019, I walked over to the Rayburn House Office Building for a hearing with the CEOs of the nation's three largest credit bureaus. This was my first opportunity to question corporations that dealt with consumers. Holding my half-melted iced coffee in one hand and my briefcase in the other, I rushed across the street to the committee room. I still had not relented and purchased a winter coat, and my scheduler had not allowed enough time between events. Both facts motivated me to hurry.

My legislative staffer, Kaylee Niemasik, kept pace next to me, which in her trademark heels was impressive. Some days, I'd walk even faster than needed to make the point that shoes should be practical, but the lesson had not stuck. Kaylee carried hundreds of pages of pleadings filed by attorneys representing the credit bureau, Equifax, in litigation. She was so obsessively checking her phone for updates on whether it was my turn to speak in the hearing that she nearly clocked herself on the stately marble column at Rayburn's entrance.

We found a spot among staffers on the couches in the anteroom, which is Congress-speak for a waiting room. I reviewed our plan of attack for the hearing. Committees have hearings every week or two, where invited witnesses give testimony on the topic and members can ask questions. This was my second hearing, so I reviewed the procedures, as well as my research on credit reporting.

After opening statements and witness testimony, each member, in order of seniority, alternating between Democrats and Republicans, is allowed five minutes to speak. As a newly elected member, my turn came hours after the start. I stayed hyper-focused in the anteroom, running through the questions and possible answers. I didn't even help myself to a doughnut or hear the din of chatty staffers. When it was nearly time for my turn, Kaylee handed me the thick stack of papers and pointed me to the hearing room door.

Taking my seat, I looked around the room. Three CEOs in dark suits were seated at a table in the front of the room, and behind them were a dozen lawyers who could pass them notes if the going got tough. A few reporters were surfing the internet over at the press table. In contrast to the blockbuster impeachment hearings or Senate confirmation hearings with constant clicks from camera shutters, the energy in the Financial Services room that day was sleepy.

Many congressmembers begin with a speech. I did not. After thanking the witnesses for attending, I immediately asked a question.

"I'd like to start with Mr. Begor. My question for you is whether you would be willing to share today your Social Security, your birth date, and your address at this public hearing?"

After sputtering a bit, Mark Begor, the CEO of Equifax, managed a response.

"I would be a bit uncomfortable doing that, Congresswoman. If you'd so oblige me, I'd prefer not to." He gave a weak half-grin.

"Okay," I replied patiently. "Could I ask you why you're unwilling?"

This time, he spoke with more confidence. "Well, that's sensitive information. I think it's sensitive information that I like to protect, and I think that consumers should protect theirs."

I continued, "If that sensitive information were provided at this public hearing, what are you concerned could happen?"

I was playing right into his hands, asking about a subject he knew well. Calling credit bureaus is the first step after one's identity has been stolen.

Without missing a beat, he answered, "I think like every American, Congresswoman, I'd be concerned about identity theft. I'm actually a victim of identity theft . . . of someone opening fraudulent credit accounts in my name. Somehow, they got my Social Security number, my date of birth, and my address, and then changed the address and opened up the account, so I think like all Americans, we're concerned about that."

He was right, of course. To most Americans, his testimony about the dangers of personal information getting out was not new information. But that wasn't the point. I wanted everyone to hear him acknowledge the harms, in his own words.

With that context, I asked my next question: "If you agree that exposing this kind of information, information like that that you have in your credit reports, creates harm, and therefore you're unwilling to share it, why are your lawyers arguing in federal court that there was no injury and no harm created by your data breach?"

In 2017, hackers stole the data of nearly 150 million Americans from Equifax. Reporting showed that Equifax knew about the security vulnerability that the hackers exploited but took no action to protect the data. Consumers whose information was stolen filed a lawsuit; Equifax responded by arguing that consumers were not hurt by the data breach.

"Congresswoman, it's really hard for me to comment on what our lawyers are doing . . . ," he replied, causing the people sitting behind him—likely his lawyers—to shift uncomfortably.

I interrupted, "Look, sir, respectfully, excuse me, but you do employ those lawyers, and they do operate at your direction. They're your counsel and they are making these arguments in court, arguing on the record—I have the pleadings here from the court case."

Holding up the large stack of papers, I continued, "They are arguing on the record that this case should be dismissed because there is no injury and no harm created by the disclosure of people's personal credit information. Yet, I understand you, as I would, to believe that the exposure of that information—I asked you if you would give it to the committee, and you understandably said no—would in fact create a harm, so I guess I would ask you to please look carefully at what your lawyers are doing and the arguments that they are making, because I feel they are inconsistent with some of the helpful testimony that you've provided today."

That evening, I made my first appearance on Lawrence O'Donnell's primetime cable news show, *The Last Word*. In the description of the clip posted online after the show, O'Donnell wrote, "Freshman Congresswoman Katie Porter surprises a CEO witness and everyone else with her brilliant line of questioning." And I literally had gotten the last word with a CEO, something I'd waited a long time to do.

• • •

A few years before, from 2012 to 2014, I was charged with making sure that big banks kept their promises to consumers. In a record-breaking settlement to address their lawbreaking, the banks agreed to improve their practices and help people save their homes. My job, as California Monitor, was to hold the banks' feet to the fire. Each large bank gave me a designated contact person. As I reached out to set up introductory meetings in 2012, I was on the better end of a typical professional slipup: the reply chain with unintended content. I was exchanging pleasantries with David Moskowitz, a top lawyer at Wells Fargo, and down at the bottom of an email was an accidentally forwarded message to his assistant, Debbie: "Keep an eye on this one. She's sharp and dangerous."

Years later, David apparently held the same opinion of me, having texted me a congratulatory message after the Equifax hearing. The then CEO of Wells Fargo, Tim Sloan, was scheduled to testify before the Financial Services Committee. Hoping for a smooth performance by Wells Fargo, David asked for an introductory meeting before the hearing, for me to get to know Sloan, who was mild-mannered and almost shy in my office. I don't remember a single thing he said. All I could hear was the rebuke from years before, when I suggested that banks were cheating consumers. "Wells Fargo does not make mistakes."

That was as wrong in 2019 as it had been back in 2008. The scheduled hearing was because Wells Fargo had opened up bank accounts for customers without their permission, among other wrongdoings. In fact, the CEO's opening testimony used the word "mistakes" to describe Wells Fargo's past actions. But he emphasized that Wells Fargo's top priorities were making things right for their customers and earning back the public's trust.

Colleagues on both sides of the aisle summarized Wells Fargo's recent problems and asked what Sloan thought. He thanked them for the opportunity to respond. The bank had refocused its corporate culture on consumers. Risk mitigation policies were enhanced. He told the committee that he appreciated being able to describe the new initiatives at Wells Fargo to protect consumers.

I started my questioning by genuinely thanking Sloan for his patience. I had experience on the other side of the dais, at the witness table giving testimony about consumer protection. Once I had managed to go without a bathroom break for hours, at nine months pregnant, to avoid disrupting a hearing. While Sloan definitely had it easier, the hearing was stretching into its third hour. I began by making clear that I had listened to what Wells Fargo was saying, not just that day, but for the last few years.

"In November 2016, you said, 'I am fully committed to taking the necessary steps to restore our customers' trust.' You also said on a call in January 2017, 'We've already made progress in restoring customers' trust, and we've remained committed to being transparent with investors.' In your 2017 proxy statement to investors, you said, 'Restoring your trust and the trust of all key stakeholders is our top priority.' Those statements, to me, are pretty vague; they sound like they might be obscure, empty promises. Do those statements really mean something to you, Mr. Sloan?" I asked.

"They do," he answered, nodding his head in affirmance.

"Why should we have confidence in those promises, in those statements you've made?" I continued.

"Well, when you've looked at the changes that I've made since I've become CEO, you see that team members are much more excited about working at Wells Fargo. They like what they do; team member voluntary turnover is down to its lowest level in six years. The feedback we get from our team in terms of the changes we've made is positive. We have more work to do. I don't mean to suggest that we're done. I don't think we should ever be done. Likewise, our customers are feeling the same way," he told me.

Mr. Sloan looked a bit relieved that his rehearsed answers were so well suited to my questions. I was giving him an opportunity to tell Wells Fargo's side of the story.

"So, it's safe to say that the statements you've made mean something to you and that customers and investors can rely on those statements?"

"That's correct," he concluded.

"Okay, then why, Mr. Sloan—if you don't mind my asking—are your lawyers in federal court arguing that those exact statements that I read are 'paradigmatic examples of non-actionable corporate puffery on which no reasonable investor could rely'?"

As I spoke, I reached down under the bench where I sat and pulled out a poster board. The quote, in 212-point font, was printed out. I held it up and waited.

"I don't know why our lawyers are arguing that. You asked me a direct question in terms of do I believe in the statements that I've made, and the answer is absolutely correct."

At this point, heads were swiveling back and forth watching Sloan and me. I know that, because I watched the video later. At that moment, I had eyes only for this CEO. Fifteen years had elapsed since I started studying how big banks cheated consumers. I had heard excuses ranging from "The computer did it" to "It's the consumer's fault for not choosing a bank that would treat them better." But each exculpation inevitably ended with a claim that I needed to ask a boss one rung up the corporate ladder. Finally, I had reached the ceiling. I was not about to climb down.

My whiteboard's first appearance at a hearing. If you spot a problem with the visual, see page 86.

"Mr. Sloan, you are a personally named defendant in this lawsuit, *Purple Mountain Trust v. Wells Fargo and Timothy J. Sloan.* Are you lying to a federal judge? Or are you lying to me and this Congress right now about whether we can rely on those statements?"

"Neither," said Mr. Sloan.

That was a terrible answer. Wells Fargo could not have it both ways. Congress and the courts are separate branches of government. The truth is not supposed to change, however, depending on whether the government entity demanding honesty is part of Article I or Article III of the U.S. Constitution. If Wells Fargo wanted me to believe its commitment to treating consumers fairly, it could not argue to a judge that regular people should somehow know that its promises were empty.

I spoke gently, but the point was firm.

"It's convenient for your lawyers to deflect blame in court and say that your rebranding campaign can be ignored as hyperbolic marketing, but then when you come to Congress, you want us to take you at your word. And I think that's the disconnect; that's why the American public is having trouble trusting Wells Fargo."

• • •

In the days that followed the Wells Fargo hearing, a dribble of articles appeared. My hearing questions were on the radar of the expensive corporate attorneys who made a living preparing CEOs to stonewall Congress. The headlines were not subtle: "'I Don't Want My Client to Be Blindsided': Executives and Their Lawyers Brace for Rep. Katie Porter's Questions." Another article reported that the American Bar Association had an entire panel devoted to how to handle me, a first-term congressmember. At first, I was puzzled how it was news that witnesses should expect to have hypocrisy called out. Congressional hearings are high profile, with powerful people on both sides of the aisle among representatives, and on both sides of the witness table between CEOs and politicians.

While some witnesses, especially Trump cabinet secretaries, come unprepared to testify, CEOs do not. Big companies employ squadrons of lawyers who pore through documents and practice with the executives. My team was less resourced. My one lawyer on staff, Kaylee, would stay up all night digging up dirt by looking on what she called the Ninth "O" of Google. The court pleadings that we used to hang the Equifax and Wells Fargo CEOs were the products of such a search. And while the highly paid attorneys clearly couldn't match the scrappy efforts of my staffer, the problem ultimately was not about preparation. Powerful people could not answer my questions—not because they were unprepared, but because their positions were not defensible.

Two weeks after I confronted Tim Sloan, I got a call from Elizabeth Warren during my layover in Dallas–Fort Worth Airport en route back to Orange County. In my first couple of months in office, when I was still struggling to find my way around the Capitol, I had confessed to my mentor that I was also struggling in Congress to find my voice to call out corporate abuse.

"Katie!" Elizabeth exclaimed when I answered. "I think you've found your voice."

"Thanks?" I tentatively offered, as I racked my brain for what had happened in the past week to prompt this call. I hadn't the faintest idea what she was talking about.

"Have you not heard?" she continued. "Tim Sloan is out at Wells Fargo. He resigned, effective immediately."

Every customer at the nation's largest bank got a better deal when Sloan left Wells Fargo. With his departure, the next CEO was on notice that aspirational promises were not enough to right the bank's wrongs.

But corporate hypocrisy continued to flourish, even in his ab-

sence. Facebook CEO Mark Zuckerberg testified before the Financial Services Committee and, upon my questioning, expounded
that Facebook takes data privacy seriously. I pointed to a court case
in which his company's lawyers argued that consumers shouldn't be
able to hold Facebook accountable for its privacy policy.

As I explained, "I think the American people are tired of this
hypocrisy. I've been in Congress for ten months, and I have already
lost count of how many people have sat in exactly that chair and
said one thing to me and this Congress and then done another thing
in federal court."

Hypocrisy is offensive because it's just a fancy word for lying.
Saying one thing to one audience and another thing to another audience leaves everyone doubting the truth. As consumers, we put
up with being on hold for an hour while a recording repeats that
"our call is very important." As citizens, we hope Congress will call
out the hypocrisy. But when congressmembers don't see oversight
as part of their jobs, CEOs aren't made to answer, and people lose
confidence in their representatives.

My colleague—the one who said that I was doing the job wrong
because I prepared extensively for hearings—did not expose hypocrisy or do oversight. In fact, he stopped working on official business
at 1:00 P.M. every day in order to fundraise. Our job is to get re-
elected, he had told me. But a year later, he was asking for my help
in winning his race. Nobody pays attention to me, he whined, and
everybody knows who you are. I did help him, but not before telling
him that I guessed we had very different ideas about how to do our
jobs in Congress.

Exposing hypocrisy resonates with people because we all deal
with so much of it from corporate America. Reading witness testimony in the following months, I kept seeing the same tired excuses
offered to Congress. For the next hearing, I made a bingo board
with each square representing the justifications and excuses that big

corporations offer. They warn that consumer protections could cause "unintended consequences," that their lawbreaking just amounted to a series of "inconsequential violations," that regulations would create a confusing "legal patchwork," and that empowering their customers to get what they pay for would produce

I look sad because Chairwoman Maxine Waters ruled against my use of this bingo board in the hearing, calling it a "dynamic display" not permitted under the rules. I still think it is just a poster. But a cool one, so I was willing to stand in spilled coffee to take a commemorative photo.

"frivolous lawsuits." The free square in the middle of the bingo board was "corporate greed."

As Zuckerberg showed, corporate hypocrisy is bigger than banking or financial services. Whether it's Big Tech, Big Pharma, or Big Oil, if you can put "Big" in front of it, they always use the same special interest playbook to put profits first. It tells them how to avoid answering to consumers—and to Congress—and usually, it's a winning strategy. But usually, nobody confronted them with their own words and actions. I was willing to do just that.

Pushing back on hypocrisy helped me find my voice as a representative and connect my years of fighting for consumers to the obtuse policymaking norms of Washington. At the end of my first year in Congress, a spot opened up on the House Committee on Oversight and Reform, and I jumped on it. Here was an opportunity to call out hypocrisy in all industries and all areas of government. If my colleagues were content to be Vote 200-whatever, I wanted more hearings to be number 1 in getting answers for the people I represented.

5.

Flip-flops

When you run for office, one of the first things you give up is your personal social media. Facebook stops being a painless alternative to attending class reunions and a way to stay in touch with aging aunts and uncles. Those Yelp reviews about shoddy service are composed only in your head. Stuck on the tarmac, you are not going to @ any airline for help. A great hair day is not enough of a reason to light up Instagram.

Persuasive messaging or policy updates replace whatever is going on in your day that you want to share with the world. My staff and I have compromised, and I only control one of my many social media accounts. Sometimes I put aside the politics and use it just like most of you do: to get attention or sympathy, or to share pictures of my kids.

During the pandemic, I seized the only workspace available, a desk in the kitchen occasionally used for homework. It was an ordinary day, as I sat reviewing letters from constituents and trying to ignore the ruckus of my kids. When my sons entered the kitchen, though, I immediately knew something was wrong. Instead of stomping, their footfalls sounded civilized. Then, the gentle "Excuse us, Mom," in place of "MUMMMM!" was a dead giveaway. At ages thirteen and fifteen, respectively, Paul and Luke usually communicated in yells and grunts.

"What did you break?" I asked, whirling around on my desk chair.

"We'll pay for it," Luke replied.

At the same time, Paul said, "It was an accident."

They led me to the damage. At the top of the stairs, there was a foot-long hole in the drywall.

"Get your shoes on," I told them. "Meet me in the car with your wallets."

A few hours later, I posted some of my most popular content of 2021. In a year when I had pinned down Trump health officials in order to get free COVID testing, what Americans really wanted to hear was parenting realities.

Armed with a drywall saw and a how-to video from some hottie with the handle @misterbuiltit, the boys and I placed a decent patch on the wall, and I tweeted out photos of the repair. "Even Sunday afternoons require oversight and accountability . . . These aren't just professional values; they're core values applicable to so many situations."

The boys were confused about having to do the repair, I told the Twitterverse: "We thought you'd just yell at us and then hire someone to fix it," they complained, as they lost a few hours of video game time hacking at the damaged drywall, drilling to secure the new piece, and spackling over the repair.

Thousands of likes poured in. The most illustrative comment said that the thread shows "why Ms. Porter is viewed so favorably by so many, despite holding elective office." Apparently, politicians are dirty and disliked, unless they show some character in how they parent. Just like I despise corporations that try to blame consumers for defective products, I do not accept the idea that my kids' mistakes are my problem. I learned this from my mom, who could have saved a lot of breath if she had gotten "It's not my home-work" tattooed on her forearm and just held it up whenever we whined.

As I racked up political favor on social media for my tough-love parenting, it was only three years earlier that I'd been willing to take my kids' sins to my grave rather than risk losing an election.

. . .

It was 2018, a few weeks before my competitive primary election, and I was working long hours, hoping a twelve-year-old Luke could keep a ten-year-old Paul and a six-year-old Betsy alive for a half hour until I escaped from making fundraising calls. That afternoon, I did not care that the donor needed to save for repairs to their third home, while talking to me from their second home, and could not donate. I was late, and my kids were home from school, unsuper-vised. When I finally whipped the minivan around the corner, I was relieved to see the boys playing in the driveway.

"Hi, Mom!" Paul cheerily greeted me. Next to him, Luke looked happier than I had seen him in weeks. In the past few months, the strain of having lost the Democratic Party endorsement to another candidate, Dave Min, was pulling us all down. My campaign was on precarious ground, and we were all beyond ready for the June elec-tion.

Now, I like to see my kids happy as much as any mom, but Luke and Paul were positively beaming, rather than noting that I had failed to meet the bus.

"What did you do?" I asked, eyes scanning back and forth for a blink of guilt.

As I was staring down Paul, I saw Luke turn his head to look across the street at a neighbor's house. I followed his line of sight and noticed something was missing.

"Where's the sign? It was in their yard this morning when I drove by."

"Mom, it's okay," said Luke. "They weren't home."

"You took their sign," I scream-whispered, looking around to make sure my neighbors weren't in their yards where they could hear. "Did anyone see you? This is terrible."

For weeks, my suburban street abutting the University of California, Irvine, campus had been a sad sight for our family. Directly across from my house was a political lawn sign, navy blue, with a rising yellow sun and block letters declaring DAVE MIN FOR CONGRESS. Obviously, my name is not Dave Min, and that yard sign was a daily reminder that I was the underdog in the primary election.

Dave and I lived in the same neighborhood. Our kids went to the same public school. We were both professors at the UC Irvine Law School, where we both taught business law. While there were differences between us, just like there are between any two people, to

This look pretty much summarizes the dynamic between Dave and me during the primary. He's now my state senator, and I think he's swell.

most voters we were the Doublemint Twins who had gotten into an unfortunate family feud. Our neighborhood only offered a few thousand voters, but in a primary, that would be the margin of victory. The race was tight.

In one regard, however, Dave had already won. As our mutual faculty colleague crowed on Twitter, "There are more than 50 yard signs for Dave Min in the University Hills faculty community next to UCI. Not a single one for Porter."

My campaign manager told me to ignore the lawn signs and focus on raising money for TV ads. But it was demoralizing to feel like a loser in your own neighborhood. When I asked, Luke told me he took the sign because he hated seeing it first thing when he walked out the door to school.

"When I see that sign, it makes me mad," he said. "Kids at school already make fun of me because of you. Half these kids have Republican parents, and they tell me their parents aren't going to vote for you and you'll lose. I just want to be happy when I am at our house."

Kids want to be happy all the time. That is the great thing about being a kid. For Luke, I knew that surreptitiously dropping Brussels sprouts on the floor sparked more joy than eating them. But his happiness needed to yield to nutrition. I could not stop my kids from misbehaving, but as my mom often reminded me, you have to go down swinging. Luke had stolen someone's property. As a parent, I needed to march him over to apologize to our neighbor and return the sign.

I squinted across the street at the naked metallic prongs from the lawn sign base that glinted in the late afternoon sun. I took a deep breath and turned to the boys.

"I'm making spaghetti for dinner, okay?"

They nodded, surprised at the reprieve, and went back to playing on our driveway. I headed into the kitchen to dig around in the freezer for ground beef that was younger than my congressional campaign, to use in the pasta sauce. I had to consider how to handle the lawn sign dilemma.

In the past year, I'd learned that politics makes people lose perspective. Facebook and election forums were full of people accusing each other of gaining unfair advantages, sometimes focusing more on ludicrous allegations like one campaign had mimicked another's color scheme or logo than on misstated policy positions. A few months earlier, an Xbox console arrived for Luke with no card. I am embarrassed to admit that I contemplated whether it was a secret Republican recording device to track my private conversations before it occurred to me that maybe it was a legitimate gift. I, too, had lost perspective.

Sometimes it was like looking in a funhouse mirror, seeing myself in a reflection distorted by the frenzy of politics. People claimed I was unelectable on the basis of a straw poll with a dozen voters, and that Dave and I were "nothing alike," despite the similarities of our bios and our policies.

But the truth is that I *was* thinking and acting differently because of the competition. When people stare as hard at candidates as our democracy allows, you change under their gazes. The parent in me knew that Luke needed to ring that doorbell and own up to his immoral act. The politician in me knew that Luke had taken the only political action available to a sixth grader.

But if he told the neighbor what he did, word could get out. The neighbor could tell my opponent's supporters, who might seize on the stolen yard sign as the work of a political operative out to tilt an election. In the craziness of the competitive primary, even my neighbors might not see Luke as a child. My failure to raise a docile kid who blended into the tame atmosphere of suburban California risked dooming my election. I could not afford even the hint of a scandal; it was crazy for Luke to confess.

On top of that, I could not exactly claim to have earned the vote

at that particular house. I knew every neighbor on my street—
except for that one. The unhappy likelihood was that their support
for Dave Min had more to do with my neighborly shortcomings
than any policy disagreement.

"Where did you put the sign?" I asked Luke as he shoveled spaghetti into his mouth. Rationally, the sign had no monetary value,
and the election was almost over. I wanted that sign to stay wherever lawn signs went to rest in peace.

"Don't worry, Mom. I didn't want to get you in trouble, so it's not
in our recycling bin. I put it in the recycling bin on the curb two
houses down."

"Luke, I swear! Now those neighbors will know. When they go
out to put a final load in before the trucks come tomorrow, they'll
see it. And they'll tell the neighbor. Everyone saw that sign on the
lawn," I said.

At that moment, getting caught was my biggest concern. Rather
than worrying whether Luke was on the path to being a juvenile
delinquent, I was fretting that my firstborn was a sloppy political
operative.

I hatched a plan, channeling my ugly experiences with political
attacks earlier in the campaign. I had to control the narrative, whatever that meant in this context.

"We are going to wait until it is dark, and then you can put it
back, and nobody will notice," I announced.

"Except Mr. Beckmann," Paul piped up, referring to yet another
neighbor, this one a political scientist whose area of research expertise is—I am not making this up—Congress. I groaned.

"He waved at us, though, as we were putting the sign in the recycling bin," Luke said. "So, I think he's gonna vote for you." Four
neighbors were now implicated in this cardboard drama. The campaign tug-of-war had literally arrived at my front door.

Midsummer gave me a few more hours to ponder my strategy

before it would be dark. I asked myself how the ethics of failing to return the sign balanced against my obligations to my campaign employees, who would be unemployed if I lost. By putting my name on the ballot, I had duties to volunteers who had given up weekends to help, and even to voters who had already cast early ballots for me. Moral leadership is also a part of parenting, though, especially for a single mother who was repeatedly confronting suggestions that her kids were suffering because of her campaign.

"It's dark enough," I said, knocking on Luke's door. "We should put the sign back."

I opened my front door and peered up and down the street. All was quiet.

Luke started down the front steps.

"Come back," I hissed. "You shouldn't go barefoot in the street. Put on your flip-flops." I gestured at his navy sandals, abandoned by the door when he had last come in.

"Mom!" Luke said. "Flip-flops are literally the noisiest shoes. They will definitely hear me if I wear those."

He had a point. I was really bad at political subterfuge, but my parenting instincts were in overdrive.

"Now, when you get the sign, you know it has two holes, and that you slide it onto the metal prongs to stand it back up."

"Mom!" Luke protested again. "I took the sign off; I think I know how to get it back on."

This kid had yet another point. I stopped talking and peered through the little window next to our front door. For plausible deniability, I did not want to be seen outside.

A few minutes later, Luke came back. The deed was undone.

I won my primary, and nobody knew about that lawn sign. Until now.

• • •

During the campaign, people thanked my children for their sacrifices. Mostly I appreciated it, and I would poke the kids to give mumbled gracious acknowledgments. Part of me often noted that my suburban Irvine family does not exactly have it rough. The first time the kids encountered an overflowing trash can in downtown Los Angeles, they thought it was a public emergency.

Certainly, campaigns bring changes to family life. For starters, I missed an awful lot of events and family dinners. I am sure my kids made other holes in our walls that I have yet to discover. During the campaign's end, I mostly saw my kids across the room at my rallies, if at all. They knew my attention was elsewhere. Dishing out Del Taco on consecutive nights for dinner, falling asleep before I could enforce bedtimes, and ignoring teachers' notes about incomplete homework were not super parent moments.

My kids' grumbling grew louder as online and TV advertisements ramped up in the weeks before the November general election. It turns out that my biggest audience on YouTube was middle schoolers, not voters. On the rare occasion that I would pick up Luke and Paul from school, I would see kids pointing at me and yelling, "Higher Taxes, Open Borders," repeating the tagline from the Republicans' attack ad on me. My children had hoped my fame would boost their popularity; instead, it brought taunts. They were called "spoiled rich kids"—even though we lived in the same house, we drove the same dented minivan, we had less income, and now I was rarely even home to do any spoiling.

Campaign kids do not have many outlets for their frustrations with political life. While staffers may control a candidate's social media, the universal advice to candidates is to ban your kids from having accounts at all. For that reason—and because he was twelve years old—Luke could not take to Twitter to vent about politics. The best engagement he could muster was swiping the opponent's yard sign and wearing his mom's campaign T-shirt. When he complained that his sixth-grade classmates teased him constantly about how his mom was going to lose, I suggested gently that perhaps he could stop wearing his neon orange KATIE PORTER FOR CONGRESS T-shirt to school every other day.

"I'm not going to be embarrassed of my own mom!" he exclaimed. "If I won't wear your T-shirt, who is going to be willing to vote for you?" It was the same question I asked myself every waking moment, and probably in my sleep too.

Two days before Election Day 2018, my campaign manager told me I could finally stop raising money and think about the election itself. She was making final preparations and asked who I wanted to introduce me at our election night event. The thought of taking the stage to acknowledge a loss, facing the collective disappointment of hundreds of supporters, was terrifying. Winning would bring its own immediate fears, including the continued hectic pace for my family. The person who welcomed me to the stage needed to be someone I would love and trust no matter what, win or lose. But it also needed to be someone who knew exactly what was at stake in that moment, for me as a person. I want Luke, I told my manager. She was too exhausted from a long campaign to really fight me, but she dutifully raised objections including the huge crowd, the media attention, and the political risks. I did not waver.

When Luke took the stage of the hotel ballroom, it was nearly midnight, past everybody's bedtime, including his. The election results were still coming in, and the race was too close to call. I waited behind the stage, positioned carefully in between thick electrical cords that powered the sound system, in shoes that *The New Yorker* characterized as "snazzy heels." And in that stillness before I took the stage, I listened.

"Two years ago, I thought Irvine was just a place to live. A nice place, but still just a place. Then, my mom ran for Congress," Luke began. The crowd clapped.

"What surprised me most about Mom's campaign is how much I enjoyed . . ." He paused.

Oh no, I thought. Had he looked up and been intimidated at the hundreds of people and dozens of TV cameras? Was he weighing his words, deciding if he wanted to get into trouble?

Then, Luke delivered the punch line. "What surprised me is how much I enjoyed . . . *canvassing*," he said, with a big sigh on that last word. "I've gotten to know my neighbors in a way I never expected to."

The audience, who had spent weekend after weekend knocking doors and having conversations, roared. They began to chant, "Luke, Luke, Luke!"

Like a seasoned politician, he waited for the room to quiet before continuing.

"I love the way this campaign has brought people together. . . . I want to thank everyone here for that. . . . I'm proud of the fact that there are so many people who support my mom."

He stopped again. Then, with a wobble in his voice that I alone heard, he finished.

"Most of all, I'm proud of her. It's my pleasure to introduce my mom—my hero—Katie Porter."

The picture of Luke and me embracing when I took the stage is

Election Night, November 6, 2018, Irvine, California.

my most treasured artifact from my experience in politics. More than his half-completed baby book or any scribbled Mother's Day card, it's also my happiest moment as a parent. Just as he would love me win or lose, I would love Luke as my son, whether he rejected or embraced political life.

That night, Luke showed that politics and parenting are not mutually exclusive work. The public scrutiny of our election system makes my kids' lives fundamentally political. That will never be easy, but democracy makes demands on each of us, even young kids. Rather than be swept along or hidden away, Luke found ways to do politics for himself, long before he could ever vote.

My kids call me "Congressmom." It's the most powerful job that I will ever have.

How to Whiteboard Anyone about Anything

Step 1. **Work backward:** Decide what you want the person to do. Admit something? Take an action? It's a waste of an Expo marker just to yell while holding a whiteboard.

Step 2. **Let the whiteboard do the work:** The whiteboard visually engages the brain. Do math in real time. Draw a timeline. Make a chart. Save bullet points for crappy PowerPoints.

Step 3. **Control the conversation:** Somebody is going to be in charge; it might as well be you. Use pace and volume to add meaning. Only ask a question if you want an answer. Don't ramble.

Step 4. **Don't fear the silence:** An uncomfortable silence is the sound of victory. Ask a question, then stare into your victim's soul as if you are going to reach in and rip out the answer. Wait for it.

Step 5. **Be fearless:** You have a whiteboard; they have excuses. Accountability is a virtue. Get that clear in your head, and you won't need to raise your voice or rant.

Sample Whiteboard

My son Paul tries to negotiate a raise for his weekly allowance of $7.50 for laundry because he's being "exploited."

Collect laundry:	2 minutes
Pour detergent, hit button:	1 minute
Move laundry to dryer:	1 minute
Empty dryer into basket:	2 minutes

6 minutes per load
x 4 loads per week

= 24 minutes per week

Paul's weekly allowance: $7.50
His allowance as an hourly wage: $18.75/hour
Federal minimum wage: $7.50/hour

Questions:

- Paul, is your chore equal to the labor of harvesting vegetables in the sun? Scrubbing the floor in a mall?

- Worker exploitation is a real problem. Paul, will you donate your allowance in excess of the minimum wage to a food bank? No? You ready to go do some laundry?

6.

One More Word

My mom tells the story as one of suffering, but you can hear the pride in her voice. The summer before I entered kindergarten, I was pretty big for my britches. I had a brother to boss around, just eighteen months younger than me, and free rein to run around our farmhouse and yard.

Our house was hot that sticky July evening, and my mom had barely eaten two bites of her dinner. I loved to rock back in our antique dining room chairs, having discovered that if I kneeled, I could really get some momentum. Once again, I was told to sit on my bottom.

"Why?" I taunted, anticipating what would come next.

"Because I said so," said my mom, a parenting mantra she used well into my adulthood.

My knees dimpled from the woven cane chair seat. I wasn't comfortable but I was having fun, swaying back and forth, hanging on to the table's edge for balance.

"Well, I say no." I was pushing my luck, but I wanted to be excused from the dinner table anyway. The tater tot casserole had only one tasty part—the tater tots—and I had eaten those, leaving behind the green beans and hamburger floating in cream of mush-room soup.

"That's it, Katherine," my mom snapped. "Go to your room."

My dad looked up from his plate, just long enough to register his support for this discipline.

I went to my room, stretching out on the Sunbonnet Sue quilt that covered my bed. My brother, Jacob, and I shared the second bedroom in our little house, and I luxuriated in being alone. That guy liked the tater tot casserole, but only because he was too young to know better.

A bit later, I wandered out of my room, which opened right onto the shag-carpeted living area.

"Where do you think you are going?" my mom asked.

"It's dessert time," I replied. Having pulled on a cotton night-gown, I could easily have a piece of apple crisp without worrying about my shorts feeling tight.

"Go back to your room," my mom said. "We did not say you could come out."

"But you didn't say I had to stay in," I argued.

"Go back to your room. No more back talk."

"You didn't say how long to be in my room, so I can come out whenever I want, and I want to come out now."

"You heard your mother. Go to your room," my dad said. His involvement was a sign that I was probably not going to win this round. I looked for help, or at the very least a distraction. Jacob sat in a corner sending Fisher-Price cars down the ramp of a plastic toy garage. He was an unreliable ally, leaving me outnumbered.

But I was going to end this on my own terms. I pursed my lips.

"Did you hear me? Go to your room. Not one more word!" my dad thundered.

"Okay," I replied, looking him dead in the eye.

"Goddamnit, Katherine Moore Porter, I said not one more word."

"Okay," I said again, not moving an inch.

A few seconds later, I was definitely moving—right back toward my room. My dad scooped me up, swatted my butt, and sat me down squarely in the middle of my bed.

"Now, not one more word."

"Okay," I mumbled softly.

He glared at me, threw his hands in the air, and banged the door shut. "Okay" was not much of a word, but I had gotten it in. I slept in triumph. Although I was technically in trouble, I must have sensed that my mom admired my willingness to stand up for myself, even if it wore her out.

• • •

Not all toughness is born of hardship; some of it is just hardwired. I was a determined little kid. Jacob, on the other hand, was a gentler soul. But I toughened him up in his early years, so that by the time our younger sister, Emily, was able to get in on the action, Jacob was a challenge too.

These photos perfectly illustrate my relationship with Speaker Nancy Pelosi.
They also show that I was a stubborn toddler.

Puberty came early for me, at age eleven. As a nine-year-old boy, Jacob saw vulnerability in my development, and he joined forces with Emily, who at four years old was thrilled to be included. Together, they formed the My First Bra Club.

The flag flew above the oak ball-post that was the corner of Jacob's bed: my JCPenney white bra, with little pink, yellow, and green daisy embroidery stitched to its elastic middle, duct-taped to a wooden dowel. Jacob had a captain's bed, with drawers underneath, creating a perfectly lofted and secluded hideout. This was the clubhouse of the My First Bra Club, out of reach of my angry hands and allowing for some privacy to discuss the scandal of their sister wearing a bra.

Emily and Jacob would wave the flag to their rallying cry, "My First Bra! My First Bra!," and the club would come to order. But what exactly went on besides stealing my bras and waving them around is lost to history. For me, the enduring sin of the My First Bra Club was not them body-shaming me, but that they didn't even get enough from it to be able to recall its activities. When I torture, I mean question, witnesses in Congress, I make sure that it's memorable for me—and for them.

There was revenge, of course. When Emily was five years old, my mother purchased her a book with pictures substituting for some words. A drawing of an eyeball appeared to replace the letter *I,* and a drawing of a honeybee for the word "be." This is called "rebus reading," and it's apparently developmentally normal. Jacob and I were fluent readers, however, so we started our own club with the sole purpose of excluding Emily, whom we called a "Rebusser." She claims this scarred her, but I think this ability to defeat attackers helped her beat cancer twice by age forty. 👁 + ❤️ + U, Emily, even if you still can't read as well as me.

To be clear, these fragile sibling alliances were devoid of any lasting loyalty. When we were tweens, our dad gave us each a

Valentine's Day card. I opened mine to find a crisp $100 bill, an unthinkably large amount for a family that stopped along the road side to pick up cans for nickel deposits. The card's only message was *Love, Dad* but there was a PS: *I only had enough money for you, so don't tell your brother and sister.* I quickly hid my $100 bill in case my siblings were watching, blushing with pride at being my dad's favorite. About three seconds later, Jacob yelled, "Dad gave me one hundred bones, you losers."

Falsely believing that Emily and I were left out, Jacob taunted us with his triumph. Maybe as the middle child, he needed to be the favorite when he could. But his behavior offered a critical insight for who I should trust later in life to oversee my hospice care. Hint: It will be the member of My First Bra Club *not* named Jacob. (But he can manage my money any day.)

That was one competitive kid. In our family, nature and nurture spread that trait widely, however, so I guess I cannot complain. I'm certain that the origin of the grit that I bring to my campaigns traces back to an overturned Monopoly board, after allegations of cheating or frustrations at losing. Of course, I'm talking about others losing (and yes, I was always the banker).

I assumed all families jostled for position like we did, with siblings besting each other and parents creating a dynamic where you had to watch out for the tricks and twists. Later in life, I learned that some people have families that reassure them when they are vulnerable and create homes that are emotional safe havens. This is not how the Porter family rolled. At our house, you had better stay vigilant or you'd miss out on hijinks or risk being on the losing end. Even today when we gather for vacations, "You snooze, you lose" is the family motto.

• • •

When I was in junior high school, my mom put her foot down with my dad.

"We are broke. I can go get a job and put food on the table," she said. "But you have to stop losing money."

My dad wasn't a gambler; he didn't embark on ill-fated business ventures. He was just a family farmer in the 1980s, when crop prices tumbled and land values plummeted. Combined with higher interest rates, the effect, as my mother saw it, was to throw good money after bad until we had no money at all. My mom took a job teaching high schoolers, and my dad went to work for the community bank. Everyone's loans were delinquent, and my dad spent most of his days having hard conversations.

His job was to collect the collateral on unpaid loans, and Friday afternoons were "repo" days, to get cars from struggling borrowers. In our small town, everyone knew my dad and why he was there, so most folks just handed over their keys. The town didn't have any secure parking (heck, it didn't even have a parking lot). The solution was for my dad to store the cars at our house fifteen miles away, driving them occasionally until the vehicle wholesaler came through town each month.

When my dad pulled up one Friday afternoon in a boxy gold Oldsmobile Delta 88, I expected him to have the grim face of someone who delivered bad news for a living—because that was what bankers in farm towns in the 1980s did. But he jumped out, jubilant, waving for my sister and me to come over.

"Katie and Emily, this is a great car," he said conspiratorially.

We stared at the rust starting to eat away the fenders, a casualty of ice melt and Iowa winters, and wondered what my dad was up to. A man whose birthday was April Fool's Day, he was a perpetual prankster, and that twinkle in his eye didn't come from the joy of working at the bank. He enlisted the two of us in his plan, and after dinner we all piled in the car for a drive during the long summer sundown.

After the scuffle among siblings over which of us could claim the coveted window seats, we headed out. Jacob landed in the middle, in the uncomfortable "hump" seat, but this allowed him to take turns annoying Emily and me. When the fighting broke out, my dad responded right away. Normally he ignored us, turning his hearing loss from decades of working with farm equipment into a parenting strategy.

"Katie, stop bothering your brother," he said. "Or there will be consequences."

"But Dad, it's Jacob's fault," I whined.

Jacob smirked and gave me a shove, and I shoved right back.

"Katie, I warned you," my dad said. "You are getting the shocker." He reached up and pushed a little red button, just as he had planned.

The black box sitting behind our heads in the rear window buzzed and lit up with a red light.

I screamed and writhed in my seat. "Stop, Dad, please, please, it hurts. I'll be nice to Jacob."

He again punched the button, which had wires spiraling out into the car's dashboard. The "shocker" went quiet and dark.

My parents never cared who started the fight or who was right. The problem was that our fighting bothered them, not that one of us was being wronged. Like old-fashioned sheriffs, they kept the peace but did not adjudicate blame. So it was rare that Jacob would be declared innocent while I solely suffered punishment.

Jacob gloried in the moment, and then started in on my sister, de-pantsing her Cabbage Patch Kid. She squealed, and my dad came down on her.

"Emily, share your doll. He isn't hurting it."

It didn't take much of a sophisticated plan to count on Emily being dramatic, and she struggled to regain the doll, or at least its dignity, by pulling up its pants.

"Emily, knock it off. I cannot drive with you wiggling back there. You get the shocker!" yelled my dad. He punched the red button, and again the box glowed red.

Emily yelped. When he punched the button again to end it, she popped her thumb in her mouth to soothe herself.

"Dad, what's the shocker do?" Jacob asked.

"It's like an electric fence," my dad explained, "but it's built in the seats. The shock comes from that box when I hit the button. This guy who used to own the car had three kids who couldn't behave, so he had it installed."

Jacob started to wiggle.

"Maybe I should test it out," he offered.

"But son, you aren't doing anything wrong. You always say your sisters are the problem," Dad reminded him.

"Dad, I need the shocker," Jacob said. "Come on, I can take it. Give me the shocker, please."

We were approaching our farm and the end of the drive. Jacob gave it one last try.

"It's not fair!" Jacob shouted. "Katie and Emily get everything, and I get left out. I want the shocker; I deserve it." He alternated jabbing Emily and me in the arm, as we twisted away.

As the rest of us got out of the car, Jacob stayed buckled in the middle seat.

"Just do it now, Dad. It'll just take a second."

"All right, Jacob," Dad relented. "Ready?"

Once again, he punched the button. The box buzzed, and Jacob gripped the upholstery to steel himself. That is, until he pleaded, "Dad, it's not working. I don't feel anything. Try again!"

Three of us doubled over in laughter. "Jacob, it's a rear-window defroster that the guy added to the car," Dad explained, as Jacob snarled disapprovingly and stomped off.

My dad's prank illustrated that Jacob's misbehavior was driven by a need for attention, more than animus toward Emily or me. As a father, he could have listened to our hurt feelings and frustrations and guided us toward helping Jacob mature. But that wouldn't have been as entertaining. In the end, the real joke was on Emily and me. If it had truly been a shocker, Jacob might have behaved better in the car before the blessed arrival of our family minivan.

• • •

Our strong personalities required creative parenting and tireless work. My dad handled the former, which took about one hour a month. My mom did everything else, which took about 250 hours a month. She had a shorter fuse with us, burning out from so much responsibility.

Her parents lived in the scenic small town of Decorah, about five hours away—if the roads were not icy, if we didn't stop six times to go to the bathroom, and if we didn't get stuck behind a dually tractor on a winding road. She was miserably alone on the farm, while my dad spent all day working with my paternal grandfather. Knowing these trips were important for my mom's sanity, we kids were nonetheless complete jerks in the car. She often drove us alone when there was something to harvest or plant or water or feed on the farm. When my dad could make it, we showed our appreciation by still being complete jerks in the car.

One July day, during the quiet farming week between baling hay and spraying soybeans, my dad drove our twenty-year-old hand-me-down Cadillac on the journey to Decorah. For about three hours, we lived up to the nicknames he gave us: Bitch, Whine, and

Moan (I bet you can guess which one I was). Unexpectedly, he veered off at the exit for a truck stop.

"Stay here!" he thundered. He strode into the store. These were the first words he'd spoken since we left. Nobody crossed him. Why get out of the car when we could keep insulting, poking, and bugging each other?

Twenty seconds later, he came out holding brown paper grocery bags.

"Liz, give me a pen out of your purse," he said, in a tone that left no doubt he was at his breaking point. He scrawled KATIE in large letters on a bag, followed by JACOB, EMILY, and MOM, and then placed the bags in the center console of the front seat.

"The next person who misbehaves wears a bag on their head for twenty miles," he announced, looking at each of us.

We laughed, thinking that this was probably another practical joke. We waited for the punch line but the only sound was our car accelerating back onto the highway.

A few miles later, Jacob got the bag. He resisted, trying to blame me, saying that he would behave, but Dad was firm.

"I explained how this worked. Put the bag on your head or else . . ."

Watching Jacob "bag up" was one of the most satisfying moments of my life—right up until a spitball hit my cheek. Jacob had bitten a hole in his bag, chewed on the paper, and shot it at me, all while wearing the bag.

I complained. All I got for my trouble was the bag.

Soon all three kids were wearing brown paper bags. Our car windows were not tinted, and as we drove north up Interstate 35, other cars would honk or point. Was this a child abduction? Or kids on the way to a wonderful surprise? Mom told us later that an occasional parent would begin laughing when they recognized the bags as a brilliant parenting technique. One trucker gave my dad a thumbs-up for the idea and then tooted his horn in approval.

The bags were well worn by the time we made it to my grandparents' house. Only my mother escaped the paper bag with MOM written on it, something she brags about to this day.

My sister got a college admission essay out of the experience. And I got one solid lesson: Make promises, not threats. My parents overlooked more than they saw when it came to our challenging behavior. But when they said "Here is the consequence," you could bet the farm on it.

It's no coincidence that in nearly every high-profile hearing I've attended in Congress, I have told the witness exactly what to expect. Jamie Dimon, Ben Carson, Louis DeJoy, Steve Mnuchin, and Robert Redfield all had the benefit of clear expectations. So, when each left wearing the political equivalent of a paper bag, I didn't feel triumphant. I was disappointed—in their decisions, in their lousy answers, and in their brazen willingness to doubt me. But like my parents were with me, I remain steadfast in my resolve. Promises are meant for keeping.

7.

Twelve Years Old

As a professor, I had all the answers. Not only was I highly trained and studious, but I literally wrote the questions, making it pretty easy. By the time I ran for Congress, I was teaching from textbooks and teachers' manuals that I'd authored. I was firmly in control of my classroom, and when I spoke, my students paid attention. Some tried to take down every word of my lectures, and others were regulars at my office hours, hoping to impress me with their work ethic or intellectual curiosity. I was strict but fair in my grading and discipline, working to mold the students into successful lawyers.

With two decades of experience in the classroom, I expected to enjoy working with the young people who staff congressional offices. Most employees are recent college graduates, as were my law students, and I felt set up for success. With their enthusiasm and my experience, I was ready to lead our team in serving Orange County families.

House members can employ no more than eighteen full-time staffers, split between our district offices and our D.C. office. That works out to roughly one staffer for approximately 40,000 constituents. Staff handle the requests for meetings and appearances, craft and evaluate legislation, manage casework when people need help with federal agencies, write communications like newsletters and press releases, and, of course, address the ringing phones and over-flowing email inboxes.

Everyone pitches in, including me. One time, a JetBlue lobbyist called our office to complain about my tweet holding the airline to account. Expecting to reach a young staffer, he panicked when he realized his message was going literally into my ear.

"You can be assured that your message will reach Katie Porter because you are talking to her, sir," I said.

"What?!?" he squeaked. "But I called the main office number!"

The work in a congressional office is varied and requires differ-ent skills, but each office needs certain key folks. Given long, busy days with ten to twenty-five appointments, congresspeople value (or curse) no human as much as their scheduler. The job really

Reliving my intern experience on Capitol Hill, answering our office's main phone. Reflecting Congress's modus operandi, "Solving yesterday's problems tomorrow, maybe," callers had the same grievances about government that they did in 1995.

does look like Gary's on *Veep*, especially in the sense that schedul-ers are underappreciated and long suffering. My previous sched-uler, Liz, carried my briefcase, navigated me through the maze of the U.S. Capitol, booked and rebooked flights as the House failed to keep to its voting calendar, and always knew the answer to my "Who is that old guy?" queries. (The answer, somehow, was always Senator Carper from Delaware.) My current scheduler, Emily, is indefatigable; this completed book evidences her talent to carve out occasional personal moments from my schedule by squeezing more work for me into a unit of time than physics would seem to permit.

Every congressional office also requires at least one Person Who Likes to Be Yelled At. These staffers are human sandbags, and they can withstand hurricane-force gales of constituent or lobbyist blow-hards. When we get complaints about airplanes that are somehow too noisy 30,000 feet overhead, or about the lack of progress over the past hundreds of years in achieving enduring peace in the Middle East, we send in Cody or Paul. With the perfect combina-tion of charm and compassion, these staffers leave people feeling miraculously satisfied that the Office of Representative Katie Porter can do exactly nothing to address their grievances.

And while they occupy the bottom of the organizational chart, staff assistants are the lifeblood of Congress. They are human chat-bots, always at the ready to answer a phone, book a White House visitor tour, and take down your thoughts on any political issue. Staff assistants are constantly looking to get out of their chairs, in hopes of missing the daily call from "James from Irvine," who holds our office record for frequent friend, with an average of 280 calls per year. No ribbon-cutting is too small and no drive across the district is too long to deter the energy (avoidant or otherwise) of staff assistants. Often political science majors or campaign interns, these folks are in politics for the glamour of it all. Most even stay past Wednesday of their first week, when the glamour is gone. I wish them all well in law school when they realize that politics is actually nothing like *West Wing*.

Field representatives are people with serious FOMO—but they need not fear missing out, because invitations overflow any congressional office's capacity. These staffers attend roundtables and civic gatherings and annual banquets and monthly meetings (and don't even complain that the meetings have no agenda!). An amazing field rep cheerfully logs several ribbon-cutting ceremonies each month, and upon seeing a mascot in animal costume at such events, offers a hug to the furry ambassador—and takes a picture for our office Instagram. Orange County is suburban, so our field reps need to be capable drivers, unnerved by the navigation app's announcement to "stay in the left seven lanes" on Interstate 405. Sometimes field reps also have the pleasure of carting me around. I love a field rep whose driving is aggressive enough to get me there on time, careful enough to avoid my worrying about orphaning my children, and generous enough to let me turn the air-conditioning to menopausal-level frigid.

Finally, there are legislative staffers, who do the work that most people actually associate with Congress. They evaluate bills to decide whether I should become a sponsor, turn my ideas for policy fixes into convoluted legislation, and provide research and briefings to prepare me to sound, and hopefully be, knowledgeable on unfamiliar topics. As a group, these folks have big brains that seem to have crowded out their social graces. Their general tactfulness is low, sometimes approaching raised-by-wolves. I need straight answers and sharp analysis, and they deliver. In return, I try to keep constituents from entering their den, aka the "leg pit."

Staffers work long hours on top of each other in there, which gave rise to the name of their messy back office. I try to stay out of there, but sometimes I have to do some oversight. Those are some tough-love exchanges—on both sides—as you can see from our thoughts and words below.

• • •

Me: I threw open the office door and marched straight into the leg pit, not even pretending to be nice to our intern answering the phone.

Communications Director: I heard her come in to the office and storm into the leg pit.

Scheduler: The exact date was March 6, 2019, two months after she was sworn in.

Me: "People!" I said. "Do you know what just happened?" The leg staffers looked up.

Legislative Staffer: I definitely did not know, and even if I could guess, I was not admitting to anything.

Me: I was mad as hell, and I was about to drag someone down into hell with me.

Scheduler: I began scanning the calendar. Did we miss something? Did she not have any breakfast or lunch? Things were not good. I could offer her a mini Diet Dr Pepper? Or maybe some of those free almonds we get from the California Nut Association?

Comms Director: I heard every word. My office, intended as an actual supply closet, was right next to the leg pit. But she wasn't talking to me, and given the tone in her voice, I hoped it stayed that way.

Leg Staffer: The closet was prime real estate because it had a door. There was a fight over the closet, and the comms "director" won because he directed only one person, himself, so his entire department fit in there. Truly, politics is not fair.

Me: I had just come from the House floor, which meant that I was tired and overstimulated.

Scheduler: I got paid to go into the fray, so I headed to the leg pit, adding a seventh person to the tiny space. I stood behind Katie, so I could hear what was happening but stay out of her line of sight. Her face was red. Maybe she was dehydrated, so I thought again about getting that soda.

Me: "Do you all know where I was? Did you watch?"

Leg Staffer: Katie was a freshman member, and nobody was paying any attention to her at that point. The only way someone would've been watching her is if she were speaking on the House floor. I got a bad feeling.

Me: "I just gave my One Minute. And it was an embarrassment!"

Scheduler: A "One Minute" is when congressmembers can speak on the House floor about whatever they want for sixty seconds. That day, we'd sent Katie to give a speech about one of her bills, the Help America Run Act, to reform campaign finance.

Leg Staffer: "Did you not like the speech? I can fix it."

Me: "Fix it? How are you going to fix it when I already gave it? Does nobody around here pay attention to me?"

Staff Assistant: I definitely paid attention to the congresswoman. I only hoped that someday she would pay attention to me in return. Had I missed an opportunity to be helpful? Was this going to affect my recommendation letter for law school?

Leg Staffer: I am a lawyer, not a game show contestant trying to answer impossible questions. I definitely did my research, and that was a fine description of the law that I wrote. My job was to be smart. I edited that speech until eight P.M. last night. I was a workhorse. Was it really my fault if the show pony stumbled on-stage?

Me: "I was gaveled down by the Speaker pro tem, who was presiding over the floor. I was literally midsentence."

Scheduler: I tried to interject soothing energy. "Ma'am, I'm sure you did a great job for the sixty seconds you did have. I'm sure it was a very strong effort."

Me: "Strong?" I exclaimed. "Sure, it was strong, for one minute, until the gavel began to tap, and then bang, and finally pound." I had looked around frantically, then stuttered, then skipped a few sentences, and finally bolted from the podium in shame. The speech had been three pages long, and I had barely finished one page. How could anyone have thought it would take one minute?

Comms Director: From my closet, I couldn't help but snicker. Better that someone else got yelled at than me.

Me: I wheeled around to point my frustration at the closet. "You're my comms guy. Your job is literally communications. Do you know how many words per minute I speak? How many words I *communicate*?"

Comms Director: I had no idea. I'm a writer, not a human stopwatch. My best bet was to look like I wasn't listening to every word of the conversation. I put on my best helpful but clueless face, an expression I knew would serve me well in case I lost my job and needed to work in the service industry.

Junior Leg Staffer: During the back-and-forth, I had logged into the DomeWatch app, found the House footage, and seen Katie give her speech. Well, half of a speech, as she pointed out. I saw a moment to shine because I knew what had happened. "It should have been shorter," I said. "Or you could have talked faster."

Me: "That is some strong legislative analysis," I snapped. "Someone around here better figure out how to make sure this never happens again."

Scheduler: I needed a diversion to get her back on track, or the whole day was going to fall off schedule. "Now would be a great time for a break, ma'am. How about a Diet Dr Pepper?" I signaled frantically to the staff assistant to go to the fridge. "How about we add some of those little ice cubes that you like?"

Me: I was running out of steam, with shame at my speech and the resulting tirade overtaking any anger. *That soda might help,* I thought, as I turned on my heel to head out of the leg pit.

Leg Staffer: "We'll work on it, okay?" I offered plaintively, in her wake. Part of me hoped she did not hear me, because I was still trying to figure out why it was my problem that she could not talk faster.

Me: I lay on the couch in my office and closed the door. I pressed the soda can to my head and cooled off. I trusted these staffers, and they let me down. I could not possibly write every speech or have every answer. I needed them, but I needed them to get it right. I was always going to be the one standing there doing it wrong when they made mistakes.

Comms Director: Meanwhile, I pulled up the C-SPAN archive of all the speeches Katie had given in the past—all two of them, neither of which was subject to an enforced time limit. After doing some quick math, I walked over to her office and said a quick prayer for peace before knocking. She eyed me warily as I opened the door. Swallowing any fear, I announced rather triumphantly, "Congresswoman, you speak at one hundred and sixty words per minute. Here is a one-minute version."

Me: *That's a cool fact to know about oneself,* I thought. Like my staff, I previously had no idea how many words per minute I spoke, but I wasn't going to admit that. It was their job to figure it out, and they had.

Scheduler: "Good news, ma'am. You can go back tomorrow and try again and give the whole thing. It's on the calendar." I smiled brightly. It was a miracle that Katie was free at the time designated for speeches, and I was not losing the calendaring victory of the moment. I was a problem solver, a seasoned congressional staffer, and I was going to bask in it.

Me: I took the fresh copy of the speech from my leg staffer's hand

and added it to my briefcase. The next day, I delivered it perfectly, timed to the second. The staffers who work on the House
floor were amazed that I had returned to try again.

"Nobody ever does that," they told me. "People get cut off all
the time but just slink off."

I explained to them, "Well, nobody has staff as good as mine."

• • •

It's true, as my chief of staff likes to say, that my name is on the door
and I can do what I want. I am technically the boss, although I have
banned staff—in a bossy way, of course—from using that label for
me. The honorifics may go to me, but it is my honor to have their

Our team preparing a whiteboard for a hearing. From right
to left: Jordan, my comms director, who did the math to make
sure the circles were proportional; Emily, my scheduler, who cut paper
circles out of posterboard; my butt, as I did oversight.

help in doing the work of government. It's a big reversal from the classroom. The staff have the answers, and I have the questions. Without their knowledge and hard work, I can only playact as a congressmember. To get things done, I need staff.

And staff, of course, need me too. And not just for the paycheck. In a somewhat creepy way, I am a labor of their love. If politics were factory work, I would be the finished product, built to last and gleaming with polish. The staff would be welders, constructing a record of my legislative accomplishments and soldering political and official concerns. They help me rehearse questions that devastate witnesses and write speeches of the perfect length at my spoken clip. But people only see the congressmember, and not the staff. That's probably a good thing too, given their ages.

But appearances can be deceiving. When reporters try to interview me, I point them to my comms staffer, Jordan Wong.

"See that guy? He can help you."

Often, nobody can find him, despite my pointing right at him.

"I need to talk to your press staffer, not an intern," they reply.

"That's him," I insist. "I know he looks twelve years old but that's my twelve-year-old comms director. He's young but good."

When Jordan overheard me say this, he cheerfully added it to his Twitter bio: "Twelve-year-old comms director for Katie Porter."

He recently celebrated a birthday. I sent him a Happy Birthday message, and he replied asking for a promotion. "Now that I'm thirteen," he said, "I think I'm ready to supervise the twelve-year-olds."

I laughed, but it's not too far from the truth. With four years of congressional work, he is a midlevel manager, ready to be the boss. He's talented, bright, and quite experienced, despite his youth. But I hope he turns down that label, as I have done. My staff are a team, and I'm glad to be a member.

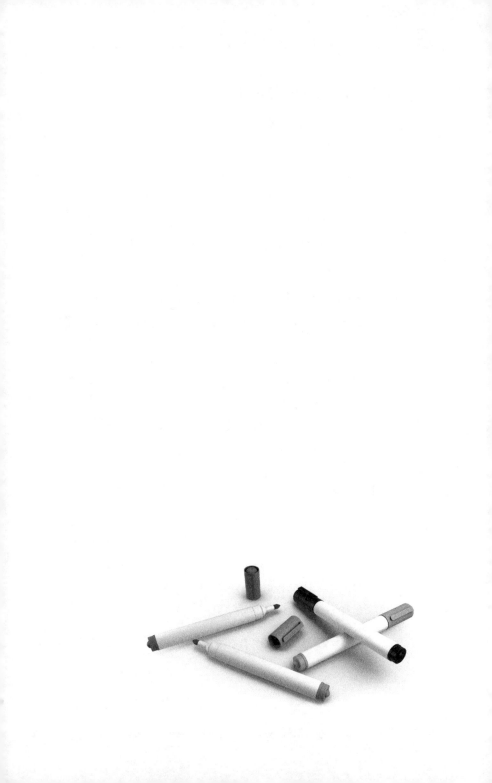

Katie-isms
(and when to use them)

My staff gives me a poster with a typo in 212-point font. The picture of me holding it up goes viral, a "paraidgmatic" example of this Katie-ism.

> **"The problem with being a know-it-all is that you really have to know it all."**

A volunteer expresses exhaustion driving me to the 7th campaign event of the day. I still have a lot of energy. Why do you think I'm the only Democrat ever to win this seat?

> **"Buy the ticket; take the ride."**

I struggle with a new whiteboard my staff procured for a video. My writing blurs, and my erasing smudges. I later discover they didn't remove the plastic wrap.

> **"Not ready for primetime."**

I'm filming a video in a grocery store about affording fresh produce on food assistance. The script instructs me to buy nine (?!?) pounds of bananas.

> **"Are none of my employees an Orange County family?"**

My staffer misstates a consumer protection law. When I correct her, she replies, "How was I supposed to know?"

> **"Read the textbook I wrote."**

My staffer grabs my arm, spilling my Diet Dr Pepper all over my dress.

> **"It's a good thing for you that I believe in gun violence prevention."**

I ask for the fourth time about updating our website and hear again: "We're working on it."

> **"Tasks without deadlines are just dreams."**

8.

Running Shoes

I grew up on a farm, a world where nearly everything required some effort. If I wanted something, I had to figure out how to get it. That meant planning, and even leaving my home to interact with people. I try to instill these values in my children. "You want Skittles? Walk down to the store. Oh, it's a mile? Well, lucky for you it's sixty-five degrees and sunny in California." If I ever catch my children ordering Postmates to get a candy bar to our home, I'll take that as a parenting failure to teach grit and hard work.

But by noon on January 6, 2021, when I arrived at the U.S. Capitol, my main takeaway for the day was that I was correct about Postmates. While I have nothing against the company in particular (and I have a lot of companies on my naughty list), Postmates and its ilk fill me with deep anxiety about the future of our world. I cannot fathom how there are now two generations of Americans who think they merit delivery of a single cup of customized coffee. That morning, I learned that not only do younger people think this, but I employed them in senior staff positions.

Early in the day, my then chief of staff, Jordan Wood, texted that he would get us coffee, come pick me up, and drive us both to the Capitol. It was going to be a long day in the House of Representatives certifying the presidential election results, and I knew I needed the coffee and the companionship. When he arrived at my basement studio apartment, his hands were empty.

"Where is my cold brew?" I inquired, trying to sound only moderately demanding.

"It's coming," he said. "From Postmates."

"What!" I exploded. "You ordered two cups of coffee delivered? Why didn't you just go to the store? There is a great independent coffee shop one block from here. You know that."

"I just thought it would be easier," he said.

"Since when is easy our goal?" I countered. "I could just walk and get the coffee in five minutes."

An uncomfortable silence filled the room. I was being unreasonable. But his actions seemed to me a clear sign that our civilization was at risk of cratering from a lack of personal fortitude.

"Even if we wait a bit here for the coffee, you'll be there in plenty of time," Jordan offered. "I'll drop you off in front of the building, so you can go right to the office."

"But aren't the roads closed, and that's why we are leaving early? There is supposed to be tight security today." I needed to be right about how this Postmates delivery was going to throw off the schedule.

"Nope," he said. "Independence Avenue between the Capitol and our office is open."

"So, the Trump protestors can just drive by and shoot us as we walk from our offices to the Capitol to vote," I joked.

My humor did not age well.

• • •

Jordan and I ended up parking and walking into the Longworth House Office Building together, iced coffees in hand. As we approached my office, we passed Alexandria Ocasio-Cortez and a staffer and waved hello. The hallways were otherwise empty, which was typical during COVID. Speaker Pelosi was preparing to gavel in the House session at a bit past 1:00 P.M. We had followed the security recommendation to arrive early to our offices.

We met up with another staffer, Nora, and started to settle into our office for a long day of waiting. The election certification process involves the House receiving each state's vote, from Alabama to Wyoming, read aloud by a designated member. Republican objections to the election results were expected for several states, necessitating walks over to the House floor to vote to accept that state's results.

I was unpacking my mom-sized tote—which contained running shoes, overdue correspondence to review from the kids' schools, stationery cards for thank-you notes to be written, and more— when someone knocked softly on the front door. I opened it, and AOC stood there, wearing a floral dress, black heels, and a long wool coat.

"Um, would it be okay if we hung out with you guys for a little bit?" she asked.

"Of course," I said, opening the door wide. "Come on in, you can hang in my office."

I offered her a seat on my couch, and my staff chatted with hers. Because of a suspicious package, the Capitol Police had evacuated the adjoining building, Cannon, where Alex had her office, so they had come over to Longworth. We get alerts fairly often for suspicious packages, so I sat in my desk chair, next to Alex on the couch, and went back to my coffee. I asked her if she would like some water or a notepad, assuming she, like me, would always have endless congressional work.

"I'm okay," she said, looking around.

I started to clean off my desk: various holiday cards from lobbyists (straight to recycling), a nice note from a departing intern (tucked into a drawer), and the expected but definitely welcome box of See's holiday candy from Speaker Pelosi (set aside for a future chocolate emergency).

"Do you have a bathroom?" Alex asked.

"Yes, it's behind that door." I gestured.

She stood up but didn't move, so I thought she needed guidance. I led her to the bathroom. She peered in and then rattled the doorknob.

"Um . . . Did you need to use the bathroom?" I asked.

"No, I just wanted to see if the door locked," she replied.

I was beginning to think that maybe I really didn't know Alex that well, even though I had talked to her dozens of times, we served on the Financial Services Committee together, and I'd run into her, her boyfriend, and their cute dog, Deco, in coffee shops. I considered her an ally and casual friend but had never noticed these odd mannerisms before (and believe me, Congress has its share of oddballs). Maybe I had let her celebrity blind me to the fact that she was weird?

I settled back down at my desk. Alex, however, was now opening up drawers and closet doors in my office. I wrestled with what to do.

If there is one inviolate rule of Congress, it is that we are supposed to honor the position by being polite, or preferably obsequious, to each other. Even internal meetings are laden with references to "our dazzling committee chairs" or "my dear colleague and friend." The jury is out on whether the American people agree, but we are endlessly reinforcing to each other that we are actually "the Honorable." Following our norm of being demonstrably collegial, I figured I should chalk up Alex's conduct to eccentricity and count my blessings that Matt Gaetz had not dropped by.

But I really wanted to tell Alex to knock it off. She should be sitting on my couch and making small talk. It was rude to snoop like this, especially when she had shown up unannounced for no apparent reason. I'm not in the running for best behaved colleague in Congress, so I offer a lot of slack in that regard, but even I was getting offended at her lack of decorum.

Alex stared into one of my big filing cabinet drawers that she had pulled open.

"Can I help you find something, Alex?" I asked, reaching to close the drawer and aiming my pointed parenting stare at her.

But I softened when I saw her face. Her eyes were wild and wide, and tears brimmed. Something was not okay.

"I'm so sorry," she whispered. "I didn't want to bother you, but I'm really scared. I need to find a place to hide."

Torn between mortification that AOC, Congress's viral sensation, could see my emergency underwear and crumpled gym clothes in that drawer, and empathy for Alex, who was crying, I decided I could solve both problems. I slammed the drawer shut and took her hand.

"We'll keep you safe," I said. "That bomb threat and evacuation must have been unsettling. What can I do to make you feel better?"

She looked wistfully down at my Tieks flats, complete with slip-proof rubber soles for the marble hallways of the Capitol.

"I knew I should have worn flats. I just felt it, that I would not be safe today. These heels don't let me run away."

Remove all the celebrity and the congressional trappings, and Alex was just another woman who couldn't do her job in stylish shoes. Today, on January 6, the job was to stay out of harm's way.

EEE! EEE! EEE! The emergency radio that all congressmembers have in their offices sprung to life, transmitting through a layer of dust. "Capitol Complex is not secure. Active threat. Shelter in place. Silence noise. Turn off all lights. Repeat: All buildings in Capitol Complex under active threat."

Our staffers burst into my office with the news. Attackers, some armed, had breached the police barricades and were entering the U.S. Capitol building. President Trump had told them an hour before to go to the Capitol and "take back our country."

"Sit here," I said to Alex, pushing her into a ridiculously huge leather wing chair. "I'm gonna hook you up."

Hopefully, the attackers would not find us, but if they did, Alex was going to be ready to run for her life. Our staff frantically scrolled their phones for information and discussed what to do, while I went into the leg pit, which was missing its staffer and intern inhabitants because of ongoing pandemic telework. I started digging through people's desk drawers and tote bags, looking into crannies. Success! I found a small-sized pair of sneakers for Alex.

I quickly returned to my office, not wanting to leave her alone. The staff were pushing furniture to barricade the hallway doors and putting the refills for the water cooler on top of chairs and sofas to add weight. They hit the lights, and I hustled everyone into my interior office.

I handed Alex the sneakers and she laced them up, shivering. I found a metallic pink puffy jacket that I keep in D.C. for the winter when I land from sunny California.

"Put this on," I told her, and put on my running shoes too.

I looked at Alex. She had found an elastic and pulled her hair up into a high ponytail. The jacket bagged around her, about six sizes too big. The sneakers didn't match with the floral dress. Alex reminded me of my elementary-school daughter, who begrudgingly wears sneakers with her flouncy dresses on days when she has PE.

Alex echoed my thoughts. "Maybe they will just think I'm a kid and not recognize me," she said hopefully.

Our plan of defense was not the National Guard or a secure office building. It was to disguise perhaps the most recognizable con-

I texted my legislative director to ask if we could borrow her shoes,
shown here on AOC's feet. Her response: "Yes. Just don't die."

gressmember in America as a child. I could only pray that it worked,
that what angry attackers would see was a lost, cold teen, trying to
make her way home safely.

"Don't worry," I reassured her, with no basis for doing so except
years of Cub Scout leadership. But I was prepared with that gigantic
tote bag. I dug around and offered her a mint, a highlighter, lip
balm, a squashed granola bar, and finally got her interested with a
phone charging cord, which she gratefully plugged in. "You'll stay
here with us, Alex. They are not going to find you."

The unspecified "they" were the people who stormed the Capitol.
In that moment, we didn't even have words like "insurrectionists"
to describe the attackers. We sat in silence, in the dark, watching on
the muted TV as rioters ran past barricades, climbed walls to enter
the Capitol, and crowded against the doors. But we had no direct
view and no information on what was happening inside the Capitol.

Every congressmember knows that it takes only five minutes to walk through the underground tunnels that connect the Capitol to the House office buildings. And I remembered that when we had entered my office building that day, there had been only one officer at the door for security.

I tried to go back to my work, opening boxes of constituent mail piled up from the holidays, ripping the envelopes as quietly as I could in case attackers were in the hallways. I sipped on my diluted iced coffee, sweating in its plastic cup. I found that box of See's Candies from Nancy Pelosi and tried to interest Alex in a truffle. She passed, as I stuffed three in my mouth in short order. We had no way to know how much danger we faced, and nothing to do to make ourselves safer.

• • •

Five hours later, we were still waiting. A few times, we heard loud male voices in the hallway. Mostly, it was silent. There was no update on the emergency radio. No phone calls or texts or emails. No police or military arriving at our door for escort. Like ordinary Americans, Alex and I could only watch the TV, which was showing violent breaches of the Capitol building, narrated by horrified commentators speculating about what might be happening inside the complex. Even though we were inside, we could only hide and wait, speculating too, on where attackers were in the building.

We awaited further safety instructions, worried that we had been forgotten in an evacuation. We debated what to do. Nothing in our indoctrination as congressmembers had prepared us for this. Our orientation training consisted of reminders that male members must wear jackets and ties on the House floor, that we shouldn't let guests use the "members only" restroom, and that we should refrain from congregating in front of the Speaker's podium. Security training was minimal, and all focused on our district offices.

At almost 6:00 P.M., my political consultant texted to confirm that I was safe: "You are finally out?"

"No," I replied.

A string of expletives, suitable for a man who had spent his life in Democratic politics, lit up the text chain. A few minutes later, he texted back: "Jason Crow knows your location and is on it." Jason Crow was not only "the gentleman from Colorado," but Captain Jason Crow, U.S. Army Ranger.

I had gotten up that morning and come in to work secure in my belief that the power of my elected office would keep me safe. I had a shiny congressional member pin identifying me as an important person in our democracy, and dozens of experiences with the Capitol Police yelling "Hey lady, stop" when they mistook me for a tourist and failed to spot my pin when I entered the Capitol. But after spending six hours waiting, I was done with the police. I just wanted Jason, who in true Ranger "Sua Sponte" style, sprang into action of his own accord to protect us.

He arrived several minutes later, a pizza in hand, and told us the Capitol Police had dozens of members gathered in a hearing room. He warned us that many Republican members were unmasked, despite COVID protocols, and that we might be just as safe where we were. He promised that when and if we were evacuated, he would make sure Alex and I, and our staff, got out.

• • •

But the next move was not to leave. Eight hours after the breach, leadership told us to plan to head over to the U.S. Capitol. The Speaker issued a call to vote. At 10:42 P.M., I stood on the House floor and voted to affirm the election results of the state of Arizona.

When we were done, I turned to exit. I was nervous being in the chamber, having noted that we had never received an "all clear" message from the Capitol Police that the threat was over. And I knew from talking to Jason that a complete bomb sweep of the Capitol, truly securing the building, would have taken much longer than an hour or two.

Tom Malinowski, a fellow member elected in 2018, approached.

"Katie, I'm organizing a letter to leadership that would call the House into a special session tomorrow morning, first thing. We have to demonstrate to our fellow Americans that we are not afraid and that the attackers will not stop us from doing the work of democracy. We cannot adjourn; we have to safeguard the House floor."

I did not hesitate.

"Fuck off, Tom!" I screeched. "We are not safe! The police could not protect us. We know nothing about the attackers and their plans. I am a single mom; I'm terrified. I don't want to ever come back here, and sure as hell not tomorrow."

I huffed off, thinking of the sound of my son Paul's voice when I had FaceTimed him earlier in the afternoon. I sat next to the toilet in my bathroom, to avoid letting any attackers know the office was occupied. I whispered calmly that it was an exciting day in D.C. but that everything was fine. But Paul, like most tweens, has a device and insufficient screen-time enforcement from his parent. He had seen the footage.

"Um, Mom, I'm a little worried," he said, trying to hold back tears. "Can you come back home right now? I feel kinda nervous." I gently reminded him that it was a long way to California from Washington, but that I would be home with him the next day.

"Would you like to go out for frozen yogurt when I get back, Paul?"

"Oh, yeah, that would be great. Have a good day, Mom," he said, sounding relieved.

Tom's letter for a special session ended up garnering sixty-two signatures, declaring in its second sentence, "The assault is not over." If I had taken the time to read that, I would have found it even more difficult to make trip after trip between my office building and the U.S. Capitol to vote to certify election results. But I did my duty that night, finally getting back to my basement apartment at 3:00 A.M.

I was bone-weary, yet wired. I had no idea where our country was headed, but I knew exactly where I was going tomorrow: home.

As our country navigated the trauma of an armed insurrection, I was recovering from a workplace shooting. In the early hours of January 7, I didn't want to play the hero saving our democracy. I didn't feel important or powerful enough to change our country's direction, only to change my direction. I wanted to be home with my family, holding my kids tight, enjoying our frozen yogurt, and lying to them that it was all gonna be okay. And that is exactly where I went.

9.

Hammer and Nails

Strictly speaking, Congress was not the first elected position that I held. From 1983 to 1985, I was vice president of the KP Club, having lost the presidency by a two-vote margin. That role went to my best friend, Angee Kerrigan, because both of us cast ballots for her as our leader. This tiny electorate then unanimously voted for me to be vice president. If today's voters had such a shared mindset, Congress would be as wholesome as the KP Club.

Named for us, its founders and initially its only members, the Kerrigan Porter Club met whenever our mothers got together. Smoking Marlboro Reds and Old Golds respectively, Liz Porter and Kris Kerrigan wanted adult time, free of their kids' demands. Our mothers expected that one playmate and the prairie would provide hours of entertainment. And they did.

The KP Club compensated for its lack of age-appropriate supervision, budget, and recreational equipment with strong imaginations and disciplined organization. As the second-in-command, I took minutes of our plans and activities, while Angee bossed our little brothers around, cajoling them until they abandoned their Transformers or G.I. Joe figures to join our activities.

Digging up dirt and adding water and ingredients like hog feed pellets and pea gravel, we crafted mud balls, recording the measurements for each recipe. The mud balls hardened in the hot sun, and we hurled them at the side of the barn, hoping to find a formulation that would not shatter. The balls that survived became our homemade weapons in the war between the KP leadership (girls) and its later-joining members (our brothers). Our mothers only cared if we broke bones, so we aimed for heads and threw hard.

Our family farm grew corn and soybeans, but its primary kid crops were mulberries and hedge apples. The KP Club had numerous meetings to brainstorm ideas for hedge apples (which the internet today advises have no purpose). We invented a variant of bowling, rolling the bumpy lime-colored hedge apples down the carport, knocking over the glass Coke bottles that our mothers emptied between cigarettes. We smashed the mulberries into pastes, creating paint for stenciling signs. Aubergine stains covered our homemade terry cloth shorts and stubby fingers, and even after a scrub with our

The KP Club staging a Little Red Riding Hood play. As president, Angee gave herself the lead, and I was relegated to wearing a ratty robe as the grandmother. But unlike Jacob, I am not about to have my head axed off.

fathers' Lava soap, our hands stayed red, irritated with mild rashes from the milky juice of the hedge apples.

Most days I was alone, separated from Angee by miles of twisty blacktop road. I would find shade during sticky Midwest summers in places like an abandoned Quonset hut that formerly housed hogs, or a secret hiding hole between stacked hay bales. Reading library books, I often wondered why the 1980s in rural Iowa were even more boring than the settings of my favorite books, the *Little House on the Prairie* series. The hottest days were a hell, and I was relieved when my parents allowed me to draw down from our water well with a garden hose to spray the hogs, and myself in the process.

Animals and their poop attract flies, and we had a scourge of them in our house, zooming past us every time we came and went via our screen door. Tired of our complaints of nothing to do, my dad hired us to swat houseflies. He offered a premium, five cents a fly, which amounted to an hourly rate likely above today's pathetic federal minimum wage, and armed us with plastic flyswatters that were promotional items from a seed corn salesman.

I focused my efforts on the screened-in front porch, since I had poked a hole in a corner of the screen a few days before, ensuring some fresh targets. Three hours later, we reported back. My dad sat drinking iced tea, while my mom fried up minute steak for dinner. My yellow margarine tub held twenty-three flies, worth over a dollar, enough to purchase a half dozen Tootsie Pops. My younger brother, Jacob, poured his flies out into a pile.

My dad poked the flies with his finger, pushing them into groups of ten for quick counting. There were hundreds of flies, and my chest heated with failure at being bested by Jacob, who rarely did anything better than I could.

"Wait a minute," my dad said. "Are these fresh flies?"

Jacob nodded. My dad poked around in the fly pile again.

"Jacob, these flies probably died last summer. You didn't kill these. Did you scrape these out of the storm windowsills?"

My dad gave Jacob one nickel for being clever enough to try to fool him, and I clutched my dollar's worth of coins in my fist. This kind of laziness from Jacob was why he could never lead the KP Club, I thought. There were no shortcuts to entertainment when isolated on a farm. Fun came only with hard work, and the only thing you could count on to pass the time was your own creativity.

• • •

My grandpa said it first, but my mom and dad repeated it, applying as needed—nearly daily.

"I'm bored," I would whine when I ran out of books.

"But there's nothing else to do," Jacob would mutter when my mom would turn the TV off, declaring that *The Dukes of Hazzard* was rotting his brain.

"We're bored," we would chime together, multiplying our pleas.

"If you're bored, get a hammer and nails and make something of yourself."

Initially, I took the point literally. With no city or county recreation services, 4-H was the only opportunity for young kids, and I logged over 100 4-H projects, from woodworking to basket weaving to quilting to baking. A partial list of my fourth-grade ambitions included: Make cookies without help, have patience with little kids, use my mom's sewing machine by myself, and ride my horse alone. I wasn't sure what my parents meant by "make something," but I had heard the "yourself" dictum clearly.

By this time, my dad was struggling to keep the farm as crop prices fell, with no lender willing to help. Scared, my mother took our family budget into her own hands and pieced together a home business to pay the bills. She taught herself to quilt and then began teaching classes and writing how-to books. Each night, I would fall asleep to the hum of her sewing machine, which was wedged in the laundry room. Her quilting business was making something of herself, and I figured the more I did the same, the better kid I would be.

My mother sewed late into the night, especially during the summer when she threw herself into our 4-H projects. We tussled over whether she was showing me what to do or taking over. (We still call our crafting projects "4-H for Grownups.") I completed two or three dozen projects each July, and quickly my blue ribbons from the county fair overflowed a shoebox.

I didn't limit myself to my strengths. The point was to do everything—just in case. Farming was not for me, but I joined the 4-H Beef Promotion Team and volunteered at the Livestock Control gate at the Iowa State Fair. My dog was a basset hound, but I managed to teach him basic obedience with the help of enough treats. I painted and embroidered, and even showed pigs. I took on leadership roles in the County Council and the State Conference. In Iowa, there were no Division I scholarships for 4-H superstars, but I took no chances in proving my potential. I was an emblematic mascot for my club's title, the Dodge Willing Workers.

In junior high and high school, I was willing to work too. Whether I was interested or talented was irrelevant because the goal was always to make the most of what was available. My parents were ample evidence to me that Future Farmers of America and Future Homemakers of America didn't offer much in the way of a future, but I won contests in both clubs anyway. It was true then, and it's true now: Nobody should have to listen to me sing or watch me compete in sports. For that reason, my parents were rarely in the audience, but they encouraged it all. My mediocrity was, in fact, the point.

"The way you feel when you run the mile and are embarrassed at your red face and dead last place is how other kids feel when there is a quiz on fractions and they study for hours and get an F," my mom told me. "You may be the best in school, but you are not the best at everything."

And so, I played the piano with no ear but with hours of practice as the accompanist at Bible school, and I suffered through four seasons of volleyball with a strong startle reflex, which had me ducking when the ball came over the net.

In the classroom I ducked in another way, hiding my grades when papers were returned and slumping lower when the teacher went looking for a student who could deliver a correct answer. My classmates, all forty-seven of us in my grade at the consolidated county school, knew that I had the answers but appreciated my re-

Clothing

Clothing Selection

Jogging Suit

For a profile of my work in Congress, *Elle* magazine asked me to model thousands of dollars in clothing. Unfortunately, I used up my hot-girl poses as a nine-year-old in 4-H.

fusal to reveal that difference. On the school bus I would shield my book using my backpack, so I could read undetected as a nerd. Homework took me ten minutes per day, so I escaped from the mandatory study halls to shop and agriculture classes.

I was academically challenged only once—in the first week of kindergarten. I came home upset after the teacher had assessed our reading abilities. To my surprise, some kids could read, while I only knew the alphabet. In a demand for accountability that I now use in congressional hearings, I interrogated my parents. They had let me fall behind right from the start. I knew they could read. Why had they not taught me?

"You're going to be bored for the rest of your life. I wanted you to have one year of school when you were challenged," my mother said.

• • •

One day in seventh grade, I was paged to the principal's office. Bewildered, I was directed to the guidance counselor, who told me that the school had a letter from Iowa State University. A professor needed gifted kids for a research project, and each public school in Iowa was asked to nominate someone for screening. If selected, I would live on campus that June and take a college-level course with other gifted middle-school students.

I took the SAT exam, wrote an essay, collected teacher recommendations, and waited. When the response finally came, I carefully used rubber cement to attach the acceptance letter to my scrapbook. I was thrilled. That summer, I wouldn't be competing with Jacob in flyswatting competitions and I could duck out on the best market hog competition at the 4-H fair.

When I told Angee, her eyes widened. A second passed. Then she doubled over in laughter.

"You're going to a nerd camp," she said. "I mean, you are a nerd, but you don't need to sign up for it."

Half-heartedly, I tried to explain to my best friend that I was not giving up my vacation for nerd camp. My time on campus would be a holiday from hiding who I was.

"I know school is boring, but nobody will understand this," Angee counseled. "You're never going to be seen as normal if you do this camp."

A flush rose in my cheeks. I'd expected her to be proud of me. But she knew the brittle boundaries of what was acceptable in our community, and that skipping ahead, and skipping out on our town, were not. Angee went on to join the cheerleading squad and stand under the lights in a cherry-colored bubble dress as a candidate for Homecoming Queen. She would wait for college to be herself. She was smart enough to know that I was different: I was a nerd. The KP Club had broken up.

No matter the number of 4-H projects, no matter that I suited up for athletics in a double-knit polyester uniform, no matter how many activities I joined, nobody was fooled. Doubling down on the opportunities in front of me was just showing everyone how hard I had to work to fit in.

When school started in the fall, nobody, not even my teachers, asked what I'd learned at Iowa State. I knew enough to volunteer only that I had seen a few Iowa State basketball players in the dining hall and was excited to root for the Cyclones to beat Kansas. Secretly, I had loved every minute in that classroom. That summer, when my freckled arm shot into the air with a question or idea, it competed in a field of other waving hands, ready to talk about the reading. In the mornings, we took a college-level course, and then, every afternoon, we were gifted guinea pigs. The researchers at Iowa State conducted experiments and tests ranging from social to vocational. One assessment determined that my ideal career was vending machine repairman. That occupation was not my idea of making something of myself, however, and I waited for another opportunity.

• • •

Classes started the next day, and we lay awake talking in the dark in our dorm room. I had made it to boarding school halfway across the country, and I was excited, pondering what was ahead and what was left behind. Sad to have no opportunity to drive after having recently turned sixteen years old, I described the perils of gravel roads to my roommate, Sybil Alexandra Burt. She responded with how her hometown of Naples, Florida, had nothing else to spend its money on except refreshed landscaping for street medians.

I didn't know how to respond. Was I supposed to be jealous or humbled? If I explained my farming community, she would not understand. Hearing more about her life would only deepen my anxiety about whether I could measure up.

Although she wrote her name as *S. A. Burt*, she said I could call her "Alex." She was excited for U.S. history but frustrated that Phillips Academy, better known for its location as "Andover," did not offer an Advanced Placement course like her former high school. I had different concerns, wondering how my math class could prepare me in just one year for calculus, a course that my Iowa high school did not even offer. She talked about the pros and cons of Choate Rosemary Hall, Deerfield Academy, and Phillips Exeter, and how she hoped that by attending Andover, she would be admitted to her first-choice college, Duke University.

"Where do you want to go?" she asked.

I had no idea, but earlier that day in orientation I had been paired with a new student whose brother attended Yale. I adopted that as my goal.

"You'll need to do really well to pull that off," she explained. "You probably don't know this, but we are already behind because we are only going to be at Andover for two years. We only have one year to get our applications ready."

Alex asked me why I chose Andover for boarding school. It was the only place I applied, I said, deciding a short response was less risky. The longer story was that the Iowa State researchers were conducting a longitudinal study on giftedness and had continued to send surveys to me in the years after "nerd camp." In a tomato red soft-bound book, *Opportunities for Gifted Kids,* I had circled every summer camp that offered financial aid. I wrote postcards asking for applications to be sent to Rural Route 127, Lorimor, Iowa 50149. Andover responded with information on its boarding school rather than its summer session. I had gazed at the course list with wonder: an ethics course on law and morality, an English course on feminist literature, a visual studies course that included color theory. I sent in my application.

When I was admitted, Angee promised to write to me. She worried about my decision, and said kindly but firmly, again and again, that she was going to "be normal" and wait for college to leave her family and our town. The closest image we had to what boarding school might be like was the 1980s sitcom *The Facts of Life,* about girls living in a dormitory with their house mother. With her blonde layered cut, Alex, my roommate, did seem a lot like Blair, the spoiled star of that show. I guess that made me Natalie, the naive, chubby brunette. Angee's letters, and those from my family, helped with the homesickness in the next year.

My mom had encouraged my interest in Andover; she herself wanted off the farm, but if she was stuck, she viewed it as a partial success if I broke free. My dad didn't see why I couldn't find satisfaction in excelling at my Iowa school.

"The highest grade at Andover will still be an A, Katherine," he said, suggesting that the issue might be my internal aspirations, not my external situation.

He was wrong about the grades. (I still ponder whether he was correct in his judgment of me.)

At new student orientation, Phillips Academy laid out its grading scale. Top honors was a 6; the minimum grade was a 1. Under the comforter that my mom and I had sewn a month earlier as my last 4-H project, I prayed hard that first night at Andover for 3s in every course, the minimum average to remain at the school. Massachusetts was a long way from Iowa, and I had traded my hammer and nails for pencils and books. But I knew that making something of myself meant succeeding at Andover, and I intended to do exactly that.

10.

Katie and the Chipmunks

She made a glamorous impression when she arrived, striding confidently into the church basement, trailed by a couple of California Highway Patrol officers for security. She smiled, shook a few hands, and began. Sincere and direct, she thanked the housing counselors gathered at the AME church in Los Angeles for their dedicated hard work in helping families victimized by predatory lending. Although it was both literally and figuratively a round-table, she was clearly seated in the place of honor.

In April 2013, Kamala Harris, then attorney general of California, was going on a victory tour. The nation's five largest banks had signed a record-breaking deal to stop their unfair practices and help struggling homeowners. Kamala was fearless for the people of California, withdrawing from the talks when she believed the other attorneys general were negotiating too few foreclosure-prevention dollars. She called the bluffs of Bank of America, Wells Fargo, and JPMorgan Chase. She outmaneuvered their army of expensive lawyers with her political will.

But even the billions of dollars in promised help were inadequate to appease the housing advocates seated at that table. For years they had raised flags, including to the California attorney general's office, about mortgage companies cheating homeowners. In 2009, in his first month in office, President Obama had announced a plan to help ten million homeowners, but four years later, just over 16 percent had received assistance. Even the negotiation of the attorney general's touted settlement had taken years. During that time, the housing counselors in this church had delivered bad news to thousands of homeowners facing foreclosure.

The advocates doubted whether banks would change their abusive practices. No matter how impressive the deal, they'd spent years watching banks ignore the terms of loan contracts and foreclose in violation of existing law. Kamala listened sympathetically, making clear she understood the stakes for homeowners, especially low-income families and people of color. "Yes, yes, exactly," she said, in response to their concerns.

The implication was clear: *Somebody needs to do some work.* But when Kamala left exactly thirty minutes later, exiting as purposefully as she had arrived, it was clear that it wasn't going to be her.

Two weeks earlier, Kamala had entrusted me to be her watchdog and deliver for California homeowners. I would "monitor" whether the banks kept their parts of the landmark deal, and this meeting was a handoff of responsibility. She expressed confidence in me to act on her behalf, gesturing toward me at advocates' questions and saying that I would follow up.

When she left, the atmosphere in the church basement soured further. Arms crossed; people tilted back in their chairs. A few advocates simply stood up and walked off as I reached for the microphone. I was a university professor from suburban Orange County and one of the only white people in the room. Worn out and broke from shoestring funding, the nonprofits were furious that not a single dollar from the banks was slated to support their work. I put my legal pad in front of me and began to address the frustrations they raised. I took down every word they said and kept at it, letting anyone who wanted to interrupt me or echo other advocates do so. When I asked if there were any more questions, I waited through silence to make sure every voice had an opportunity.

That day, at the outset, I had no staff, no budget, and no track record with Californians. I had Kamala's confidence and a two-month-old baby at home. On March 16, 2012, when my role as monitor for the California mortgage settlement was announced, I received ninety-two calls from homeowners asking for help, some with foreclosure sales in the next few days. It took me weeks to return those calls, and months to persuade the housing advocates that our attorney general had beat the banks. It would take me years to change the banks' practices.

But the strategy was right there in the press release announcing my role as foreclosure monitor: "I will work hard . . ." said Professor Porter.

• • •

In those first weeks of government service, I was distinctly *not* fearless. I was so intimidated that I implored my assistant, Lynh Tran, to attend the introductory meeting that I had with the big banks. Until she walked into that room, she was shared support staff for me and five other UC Irvine faculty members. Her background was in administrative work for the fiction and creative writing program. I didn't volunteer this fact when I introduced her as "my colleague" to the teams from Bank of America, Wells Fargo, and JPMorgan Chase.

The conference room contained no color except the endlessly compatible neutrals of bankers' and lawyers' business suits. Sitting opposite us at the expansive table were a dozen people sent by the banks, with titles ranging from the official "Senior Vice President" to the unspoken but obvious "Wall Street Lawyer Who Bills More Per Hour Than the Average American's Weekly Income." The banks described how they were committed to improving and doing right by their customers, and they reinforced each other's points. These guys were clearly on one team, and my sidekick Lynh and I were on the other.

The lawyer serving as Bank of America's outside counsel was my peer. We were both a few years shy of forty, with the same intimidating degrees from expensive schools. But Mr. Martin J. E. Arms, of the corporate law firm of Wachtell, Lipton, Rosen & Katz, had one thing that I coveted: a hardbound copy of the National Mortgage Settlement. Somewhere in the backpack at my feet were a dozen double-sided pages of the settlement, which I had hastily printed out at home that morning. Martin had all 310 pages of the nation's largest consumer protection judgment, complete with custom-printed divider tabs and a reference index.

Like an envious kid, I blurted out, "Wow, that is so cool. Could I see it?"

"I would prefer not," came the reply, in Martin's faint British accent. "But it would be my pleasure to send you one to have."

My job was to hold the banks' feet to the fire, and in the first minutes of the meeting, I was revealing a weakness by asking a favor. But I couldn't enforce the settlement on such an uneven playing field.

While the banks had paid billions to the state, California's then governor Jerry Brown used nearly all the money to plug a hole in the state budget. To fund my work as monitor, Kamala had fought to set aside a small fraction of the banks' fines. When she called to recruit me to be monitor, at the recommendation of Elizabeth Warren, Kamala was honest. I still have my scrawled notes, and they include the phrases *resources are pretty limited* and *labor intensive position.*

Lynh made a convincing faux regulator that day. More important, she had unparalleled organizational skills, wading each day through dozens of long voicemails and boxes of loan documents that homeowners sent us for review. I put her on my payroll and, out of desperation, hired the only other help I could find: Alvin, Simon, and Theodore.

The "Chipmunks" were law students between their first and second years, earning their nicknames because they were kids with big hearts who caused me trouble. And like their rodent counterparts, each of the trio had different talents. Alvin was confident and a risk-taker, formerly a professional extreme skier. All summer long, he kept insisting that he could beat the banks, if only I would trust him. Simon was a nerd who memorized much of the three-hundred-page mortgage settlement. And Theodore was so gentle and kind to the stressed homeowners who called, naively believing we could help everyone.

With only one year of law school complete and transcripts full of B grades, the Chipmunks were not exactly intimidating. But their shenanigans quickly unnerved the banks' highly paid lawyers and "dedicated customer relationship managers." They made a three-way call into Bank of America's "hotline" with a homeowner, only to hear the bank employee misrepresent herself as a U.S. Department of Justice agent who was purportedly required to administer a lengthy "consumer survey" as a condition for helping the homeowner. They waded through hundreds of pages of correspondence, finding outright lies and illegalities. On phone call after phone call with the banks, they documented dizzyingly bad and inconsistent communication that the banks had sent to homeowners.

Rather than bemoan the overwhelming number of homeowner

complaints, I saw each new request for help as another piece of evidence with which to build a case that the banks needed to do more. Together, the Chipmunks put every action of the banks dealing with homeowners into a database. The pulldown menu of lawbreaking was long: *bank lost documents, bank lost documents two or more times, bank never called back, bank misstated the law, bank failed to evaluate homeowner eligibility for help, bank required paperwork to be sent by fax, bank agent claimed to have no supervisor,* and my personal favorite—*bank computer made a mistake* (the corporate equivalent of "dog ate my homework").

With the Chipmunks at my side, I quit wasting my time in fancy conference rooms, hearing bankers recite their narrow interpretations of the law, and I started looking exclusively at what was happening on the ground in California. I hired a half dozen newly minted lawyers to keep wading through the hundreds of homeowner complaints that arrived each month and to return every call from homeowners and advocates.

We started to beat the banks. On October 12, 2012, a couple in Oakland received a letter forgiving $496,407.53, the full amount of their second mortgage. Just before the mail was delivered that morning, the house had been sold to pay off the delinquent loan. Bank of America said it was out of its power to reverse the sale. We retorted that the bank surely did have the power to transfer money, if not the property, and got the family a six-figure compensation check. When Wells Fargo argued that it couldn't split data by zip code to verify that low-income neighborhoods were getting equal settlement resources, I noted that even the Chipmunks, who were math-challenged law students, knew how to sort a database. We caught Chase Bank forcing consumers to sign away their rights to sue for legal violations in order to be considered for mortgage help. We forced them to send hundreds of thousands of correction letters, "apologizing for the inconvenience" of the bank breaking the promise it had made only months before in the settlement.

I developed a taxonomy for how banks responded to our calling out their misconduct. Bank of America was incompetent, Wells Fargo was an asshole, and JPMorgan Chase was an incompetent asshole. It was not my kindest moment, but I wasn't wrong. One bank executive wryly noted that I was a "very unusual regulator." When I asked what that meant, he said that after lodging a complaint, I would follow up again, and again, and again. And, he sighed, "you complain about everything."

"Don't make mistakes about everything," I replied.

• • •

Kamala had brilliantly understood something that few government officials ever do: The victory is not the press conference and the promises, but actually changing people's lives. When she hired me, she was clear that I should look at the data to verify that the banks were helping people avoid foreclosure. But not even the attorney general expected how dogged we would be, creating data of our own.

Every word that a bank executive said to us was documented, and soon the greatest hits written on yellow sticky notes covered a wall. I still have them, and they still spark a combination of laughter and outrage.

- "I don't have any answers for you today, unfortunately."

- "I think I may have dropped the ball on this."

- "I wonder if we could just start over."

- "I don't want to make anything up, but . . ."

- "I think this one is my fault."

- "I confuse myself sometimes."

- "I don't want to say because I don't know."

The challenge for the banks was that *we* did know. They weren't used to that, even from government officials who were supposed to enforce the law. My authority was limited to California, however, and Kamala had created my position without getting the banks' agreement. The banks had negotiated only for a national monitor, choosing an older Southern white man, with decades of experience as a bank examiner. He refused to take any calls from homeowners. When I prevailed on him to come to California to listen to the stories of foreclosed homeowners, he told them he knew the pain of home loss. Just a year before, in 2011, Hurricane Irene had destroyed his yacht in North Carolina.

I had a different set of real-world experiences to bring to the job, having grown up in the throes of the farm crisis, and having for years studied families in bankruptcy. At every opportunity, I got more firsthand evidence of fallout from the foreclosure crisis. Complaints were coming in from cities about foreclosed homes ("REOs," in the terminology that stumped Housing Secretary Ben Carson) that were in serious disrepair, creating dangerous conditions and lowering property values. Urban communities of color had suffered for years, and the mortgage settlement addressed the issue: "Servicer shall develop and implement policies and procedures to ensure that REO properties do not become blighted." The national monitor asked the banks if they had developed and implemented policies and procedures. *We sure did,* the banks told him. And that was that.

But when I asked about these policies and procedures, the banks refused to give me any information on blight prevention, citing the national monitor's satisfaction. The rules applied in California too, and in asking homeowners, not bankers, how things were going, I got a different story. On a conference call to address the conditions of a home in the San Fernando Valley, one lawyer began by reciting the bank's records of routine property inspections. Since the property wasn't blighted, he explained, there was no need to even argue about the bank's obligations to address blight under the terms of the mortgage settlement.

"Could you wait just a minute?" I asked. "Okay, can you take a look at the email I just sent?"

Silence.

"Did you get it? Any problems opening the attachments?"

Earlier in the day, my staff had driven up to Los Angeles to take pictures of the house. And they were not pretty.

The next day, the bank had contractors on-site, boarding up the windows, cleaning out drug paraphernalia and animal droppings, and picking trash out of the yard.

• • •

My approach to oversight got noticed. A newspaper headline described California as "The State That Ate the National Mortgage Settlement" because banks were focusing so much attention on our demands. I received awards, including for being one of the Best 100 Lawyers in California, and some plaques now taking up space in a box in my garage. I was named one of the Hot 100 People in Orange County, an honor based on my work as a foreclosure fighter, not my appearance. And, while I am not a fan of smashup words, I nonetheless appreciated the InnovAction Award from the College of Law Practice Management; "innovation" and "action" being associated with a government program was surely a win.

The most amazing thing about our success, however, was that I had zero actual legal authority. The banks had explicitly refused to agree to a monitor for the state of California. In her own words, Kamala had "gone rogue" when she appointed me. I had her force of character behind me, but no legal rights. But consumers never have as many resources or as much power as corporations, and the scale of a crisis is always overwhelming. These circumstances combine to leave people doubting whether government cares about their problems.

A decade later, the man who had been Kamala's top advisor when she was attorney general was interviewed for a profile about my oversight work in Congress. He was asked how I'd managed as monitor to beat the biggest banks in the country, without wielding a whiteboard or having congressional hearings or legislative authority. He gave a few examples.

"Then," he continued, "there's the follow-up. Katie is the master of follow-up. She outworked the banks. She just outworks everybody."

That's probably true, but there's more to it. Not owning a yacht also helps.

11.

Spam, Not Scam

At the risk of unleashing malware upon my two-decade-old Hotmail account, I clicked on the email.

Dear Malgorzata,

 Time is running out to sign Adam's birthday card before we deliver it to him at the end of the day. Adam has done so much for our democracy and country over the past year. Let's kick off his 60th birthday right with a big show of support!

 Hi there, Malgorzata. I'm reaching out for the first time to see if you can help me with something. Today is Adam's birthday and he's 60!! I know, I can't believe it either. Given how hard he's been working to defend our democracy and support our communities through these challenging times, I'd love to give him a birthday card with as many signatures as possible from supporters like you.

If my friend Adam Schiff is reading this book, I have a couple of thoughts to share. First, my name is not Malgorzata; it's Katie. The identity confusion probably does not involve only me and my doppelgänger, Malgorzata, but is the result of a mail merge affecting thousands, so some oversight is needed. Second, not to be a prose style snob, but I have never understood why these emails have two salutations. Perhaps if this had gone to Malgorzata, it would have made her feel special. It did not have the same effect on me. Third, I can totally believe you are over sixty years old, Adam, because defending our democracy does cause wrinkles and hair loss, and you did the Lord's work for a year or two. Fourth, if anyone who purports to love me ever considers giving me a card digitally signed by random people for my birthday, know that I will no longer love you. I much prefer diamonds or flowers, or even one of those texts with the balloon graphic that appears upon delivery.

Adam, and every other candidate out there, I feel your pain with these fundraising emails. My own fundraising correspondence has had hiccups. When I launched my campaign, I downloaded my phone contacts into the finance software, and as a result, here are the subject lines of the solicitations to my mother:

- "Hey, Mom, key endorsement alert!"

- "Mom, we know you support Katie."

- "Your voice matters, Mom."

- "Mom, I'm going to keep this short."

That last one is how I try to start my phone calls with her when I'm busy in the Capitol, so it has the benefit of being something I would actually say.

These fundraising emails are hard to read and hard to write. My basic approach is "spam, not scam." Any message to a mailing list could be called spam, and I limit how frequently we reach out because even my own children complain that they get too many campaign emails. But we send a lot of emails because winning campaigns need a lot of money. So the spam aspect of online fundraising is somewhat inevitable, even with the best of practices.

But scams are just wrong. Nobody asking for the public trust in seeking an elected position should be allowed to bamboozle people out of their money. Yet, both Republicans and Democrats tell outright lies. This is shameful, it should be illegal, and I have proposed legislation to crack down on this.

As a consumer protection lawyer (and as a service to you, dear reader), I am happy to outline a few of the lies—and some surprising truths.

First, nobody is out there "triple-matching" (or even matching) any online donation, not even the Koch Brothers or George Soros. The handful of mega-donors who give billions to influence elections are not making sure your $3 donation is matched with $9 from them. I promise.

Second, nobody legitimately cares how many donors give on a certain day or how much money comes from a particular zip code. Campaigns want local donors because those supporters will vote for their candidate, but hitting that DONATE button does not tick down some magical counter from 103 supporters to 102 supporters urgently needed in your community.

Third, and perhaps most egregious, the emails that have subject lines like "Warning: Payment Incomplete" or "Final Notice #89721," suggesting that there is an unpaid bill or debt collector coming for you, are simply false. Delinquent bills are incredibly stressful, and preying on people by invoking that fear should be unacceptable—to every party, organization, and candidate.

Personally, I also despise emails that use terrorizing graphics. "🚨🚨🚨 ACT NOW OR WE LOSE!!!" in a blinking text box does not befit a country that purports to be the world's greatest democracy. I have anxiously clicked several times on emails that announce

"Katie Porter is in BIG TROUBLE" only to discover, whew, that my only trouble is serving in Congress. Groups even use my name without permission to raise money for their organizations. All these undesirable tactics flourish because they are effective. If people stop donating in response to emails like this, the fundraising will change to honest appeals that are rooted in facts.

Deceptive statements like fake deadlines, fake matches, and fake electoral losses should be illegal. But worse than scam emails are scam PACs, political organizations that exist to steal money rather than support political causes. Often employing sympathetic groups like veterans or law enforcement, or lovely causes like saving our democracy or stopping insurrectionists, these groups collectively raise millions of dollars each month and give it out—to themselves! Their expenditures are solely for inflated fees to "consultants" or "strategists" who run the PAC. The donations never, or rarely, support candidates or legitimate political action. While spam is here to stay, in both its political and nonpolitical forms, the scams should stop. I have introduced legislation to require PACs to actually donate to political causes if they solicit donations for that reason. In other words, do not lie.

We should be able to trust that our donations go toward politics, and not profit. From Malgorzata to Mom, people who donate to engage in our democracy should be safe from rip-offs. It's that simple.

• • •

For now, raising money is an inevitable part of politics. Before most candidates begin their campaigns—while they are still imagining the glory of running for office—those fantasies get upended by a horrifying political reality: rolodexing. For everyone not living in a nursing home, a rolodex is a circular desk accessory with specially shaped index cards for each of a person's accumulated contacts. The stationery product may not inspire much emotion, but let me tell you, the political act of rolodexing is both spiritually and morally demoralizing.

Here's how it works: The candidate exports all their phone or email contacts into a spreadsheet and then puts a dollar figure next to each person that represents "what you think the person is worth." That number is not how much they love you or how hard they'll work to get you elected; it is how much they can donate to your campaign.

When I started rolodexing, I dutifully put down $25 and $100 next to hundreds of people's names, marking zero for people listed in my contacts as *Tile Cleaning Guy* and *Taxi that Shows Up*. I knew twenty-eight people who I thought could give the then allowable maximum of $2,700. The sum of all the numbers, big and small, was $211,490. This final rolodex calculation was a purported measure of whether I was a viable candidate. I had sailed past $100,000, which I was told was a minimum threshold. Clearing this hurdle was easy, given that my estimates were wildly off. Even six years later, I have not gotten donations from half of my self-identified max-out donors. (If you think I am talking about you, my address is P.O. Box 5176, Irvine, CA 92616, check payable to "Katie Porter for Congress.")

One challenge was that most of my professional contacts worked in foreclosure prevention, and saving homes just does not pay like building them, buying them, or lending against them. A few months into my campaign, I stopped to soothe myself at Yogurtland. I got a reasonably sized portion of tart yogurt and used restraint by topping it with fresh fruit. As I walked out, my phone chimed. A friend who advocated for low-income housing had texted, apologizing for ignoring my repeated donation calls. He said that he would be delighted to give. I had logged him down for $50 in rolodexing, but I was struggling to raise money with a crowded primary field and an entrenched Republican incumbent. *Every dollar counts,* I told myself.

The phone dinged again, with a picture of the donation receipt. $27.00. I sighed, thinking that at least I got more than half of the $50 I had estimated he would give. And, I had yogurt. I pecked out a thank-you, squinting at my phone to check for typos before I hit SEND. Wait, he gave $2,700. I was rich! More precisely, my friend was rich. This was the largest donation I had gotten in weeks. This is also how I learned that if you want to upgrade your Yogurtland to celebrate with a bunch of chocolate and caramel topping, you have to get a new cup. And you'll likely spill it all over yourself mixing it together, but that night, I didn't care.

Because my estimates were wrong in both directions, I continued to dial everyone I knew. Again and again. I am so grateful to everyone who still speaks to me after this stalking—all seven of you. To the rest of my former friends, I cannot blame you. It's a truly broken aspect of our current democracy that raising money early in a campaign is a requirement, and the only way for a regular person to get early money is to pester the heck out of your friends. The Democratic and Republican parties not only accept this system but often recruit candidates who are so rich they don't even need rich friends. Donating millions to your own campaign is one way to avoid fundraising pressure and explains why so many congressmembers are multimillionaires—they were rich before they even got there.

Only a few organizations attempt to level the playing field and help candidates learn how to fundraise. In 2017, I was the first candidate to earn the support of EMILY's List, an organization dedicated to electing pro-choice Democratic women. You might think I am grateful to Emily, but I am not. In fact, she does not exist. The organization's name is an acronym for Early Money Is Like Yeast. When I heard this, I was excited that perhaps there would be tasty baked goods if I hit my fundraising goal. Alas, the yeast refers to the fact that early money "makes the dough rise." If a candidate can raise money in the first weeks of their campaign, they are seen as viable and having a chance at winning. People don't bet on losers, so early money begets more later money.

EMILY's List trains promising candidates to fundraise, and following their advice guarantees that you *will* raise money—and also that you will hate the entire world. To meet their goals, I would make calls until I was hoarse and out of breath. When I needed a break, I would hide in a broom closet in the co-working space that housed our early campaign, thankful to have paper towels on those shelves to wipe away tears of frustration.

I was compared unfavorably to other candidates in my area. Others were making bigger asks, pushing donors harder, knew better (aka richer) people to call. Most of those candidates were not elected, and none still serve in Congress, so I would like to say, "Phooey on you, Emily." But right after that, I would like to thank everyone at EMILY's List for having confidence in and patience with me as I figured out how I could fundraise successfully and with my soul intact.

I slogged through early fundraising. I used to think the longer I talked, the more money I would receive. This is the same problem that men have when hitting on women for sex. More self-aggrandizing stories are not going to increase the chances of getting naked. The same is true of getting a donation. If it's going to happen, don't waste valuable time. If it isn't, you're just blowing hot air.

Things hit a new low when I called my first dead person. Election law requires a donor to be alive, and the very fact that this law is necessary is a sorry commentary on our democracy.

When I called Rosalyn, her husband answered, saying that she could not come to the phone. I persisted and asked if I could leave a message.

"No, I am sorry, that is not possible."

"Oh, maybe I could call back," I said.

"I am sorry, but no."

"Well, um . . ." This man was awfully good at discouraging callers.

"She passed away," he said.

At that point, I panicked. Hanging up in horror seemed like the best option, followed by shouting, "Sorry, wrong number!" But if this call was over, I would have to dial someone else. Better the dead person you know than the cold-call donor you don't.

"I am very sorry for your loss. Did Rosalyn enjoy political giving?" I asked.

For the next several minutes, I learned about Rosalyn's battle with cancer, her charitable work to help children, and her passion for electing women.

When I hung up, I wrote a short note to her husband. I apologized for troubling him and expressed appreciation for all of Rosalyn's good work in her life. One week later, I received a check for $1,000. I still have the little note that was stuck to the check: "She would have liked you."

I think I would have liked her too. I like donors, just as much as I like non-donors who vote or knock doors or advocate for better policy or volunteer or otherwise try to make the world better. Donations, like those other activities, are acts of faith in our country. My conversations with donors are nearly identical to the ones that I have with people I meet in airports, at coffee shops, out shopping, and even when I am in the gym locker room—and yes, that is awkward. People send me notes about their fears for the future and their aspirations for our country, and I read them whether they are stuck to a check for $1 or $1,000. I hear about the costs of college or their health problems, and I listen to their frustrations with Congress ("Same!" I often respond).

People who give to me are only looking for one return on their investment in the election: a better democracy. I refuse both corporate PAC and lobbyist donations, and I am one of only a dozen or so members of Congress who turn down both kinds of money. When candidates rely on huge donations or corporate money to avoid the hard work of earning their communities' support, fundraising becomes evil. But donors don't corrupt politics; politicians corrupt politics.

When politicians do their jobs and people donate whatever they can to keep them doing that work, fundraising is not that much different from calling your congressperson or registering to vote or attending a town hall. Almost half a million people have donated to my campaign, giving an average of $20 apiece. That is one of the lowest average donation figures in recent elections, but it reflects that the business of democracy still has too few customers.

A donation, of any amount, is a decision to do something to shape our democracy. Our biggest problem is that most people do *not* get engaged, which allows the few who do to have an outsized influence. That distorts politics and elevates candidates who put donor interests ahead of everyone's interests. Fundraising is not evil if it translates into communication, engagement, conversations, and opportunities for everyone, no matter their net worth.

• • •

I called a woman from Los Angeles to thank her for her donation and asked if she could give again in the upcoming months.

"Well, I did have to recently reevaluate my approach to political spending," she told me.

"Of course," I said. "I appreciate your willingness to talk with me and understand that you cannot give right now."

"Oh, honey," she laughed.

The previous week, her longtime accountant, Chester, had confronted her about the dozens of transactions in her bank statement on a website called ActBlue. He was concerned that she had a gambling problem and might need addiction treatment. She explained that this was the online portal for giving to Democratic campaigns. Rather than being relieved, Chester became indignant, chastising her to stop wasting her money on politics.

"Don't worry about my donations," she told him. "There is no investment as good as betting on the future of America. I am going straight to ActBlue to donate my new windfall after I hang up with you."

"A new windfall?" Chester asked, puzzled but intrigued.

"I have the savings from no longer paying you to be my accountant."

As I processed her credit card for our campaign, I made a note about her donation: *R.I.P. Chester.*

Show Me the Money

Why do candidates want donations early?

Donating early helps campaigns stretch your dollars. The later you buy television time, the higher the cost and the less you get. Airing your commercials during a 2:00 p.m. soap opera for a gajillion dollars is the political equivalent of buying a $962 middle seat in row 37 on departure day.

Does the campaign really need your dollars?

Competitive races need money, but millions get wasted trying to defeat or help politicians in noncompetitive seats. Tough races typically have party registration differences of 15 points or less. Check a reputable election ratings site before you give.

How does the money get spent?

Campaigns should spend on two things: 1) voter engagement and persuasion, and 2) raising more money to do number 1. Here's a breakdown of our 2018 budget.

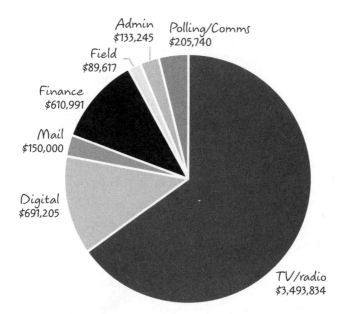

Admin $133,245

Polling/Comms $205,740

Field $89,617

Finance $610,991

Mail $150,000

Digital $691,205

TV/radio $3,493,834

Isn't it terrible that there is so much money in politics?

Yes. It's gross. My 2022 campaign spent $27 million to win.

12.

Fresh Start

I f you are under forty years old, you have likely been told repeatedly and without solicitation that you need to find a mentor. Believe it or not, people used to go through their lives without having a denominated mentor, just like they used to have to put their finger in a little hole and turn the dial to make a phone call. In college in the mid-1990s, few of us went around searching for a mentor. We just asked each other for advice, and some poor decisions and lost opportunities resulted.

When I arrived at Harvard Law, mentors were becoming a trendy must-have for every aspiring young professional. This mythical figure would help you figure out your career, encourage you, and generally guard against your parents' fear that you'd be heading back to your childhood bedroom after graduation. Mentors can definitely make a difference, but so can parents, teachers, peers, siblings, and bosses. Seeking out a specific "mentor" on top of all these others can result in certain absurdities.

As a law professor, I loved helping students find their footing and begin their careers. Their holiday cards are my favorites because their successes boost my ego; it's like bragging without being tagged as Katie Porter, Self-Promoter. And when they struggle, I get to lend a sympathetic ear and a helping hand.

But for every student with whom I had that kind of relationship, I was probably an official mentor to five others. If you are confused by that statement, you have something in common with most of my "mentees." Here's how these interactions typically went:

Near the end of the semester, a student knocks timidly on my open door during office hours. I welcome them, and they sit politely. They make a tepid comment or two about enjoying the class I am teaching, and I respond with a generic pleasantry. An awkward silence arrives.

Eventually I ask, "Is there something I can help you with?"

The student looks down at their sneakers and blurts, "Will you be my mentor?"

There is really only one answer to that question if you want to stay in the running for Professor of the Year.

"Yes, of course," I say.

"Wow, great. Thanks so much, Professor Porter. See you around."

And like that, the student grabs their backpack and flees my office. I never see them again, except in the back row of class for another week or two before the semester ends. These young people have zero plan to receive any guidance or build a relationship, so that is usually what happens.

Such interactions were largely rote and worthless, but students left satisfied, thinking with pride, *Check! I have a mentor.* I know because this scenario is exactly what happened when I asked my constitutional law professor to be my mentor.

"Sure," said Elena Kagan, then trying to get tenure at Harvard Law School.

I felt great at my success in getting a mentor and proceeded with my studies. I didn't reach out to seek advice or learn more about her interests. During my remaining time at Harvard, we never spoke again. I technically had a future Supreme Court Justice as my mentor and, due to my own missteps, I have nothing to show for it but this story.

When I tried again a year later, things went differently. I had started to realize that more was required to build a mentor-mentee relationship, and Elizabeth Warren certainly made clear in her answer to my question about mentorship that it was something to be earned. When I asked her, she replied, "Maybe. Let's see what you can do."

And then she gave me a year's worth of work.

. . .

A few weeks earlier, in the fall of 2000, I had enrolled in Elizabeth Warren's bankruptcy class. Several friends who had taken her other classes warned me, "Try to volunteer. Then she might not call on you." No one wanted to be caught off guard by Professor Warren.

To make myself extra visible, I sat right in the front row. Having carefully done the reading, I volunteered an answer. I was confident, well-spoken, and, apparently, wrong.

"Think, Ms. Porter. Think!" she said, pushing me to try again.

I wilted, and tears welled. I *was* thinking, apparently just not impressively. I had volunteered, but she still came for me.

In her book *Persist* Elizabeth tells this story in more detail. I remembered it again when I questioned Dr. Ben Carson, President Trump's Secretary of Housing and Urban Development. Struggling to define a basic housing term, he furrowed his brow and sweated. Believe me, he, too, was thinking—just not successfully. The difference between Ben Carson's shamefully wrong answers and my own was what happened next. He laughed it off, and I begged Elizabeth not to give up on my potential. She recalls my grit much more than my mistakes.

When I asked Elizabeth to be my mentor, I was chasing after her, literally. She had just taken a group of students out to lunch at Border Café in Cambridge, and I was panting to keep up with her as we walked across campus to her office. I told her I was interested in teaching law, and that with her course on bankruptcy, I had found a subject that captivated me. She responded by outlining a plan for me: I would do very well in her class. If I did that, I could help her with her new research project on why families file bankruptcy. If I impressed her with that, she would be a reference for me, and if I did about six other things like clerk for a prestigious judge and write a law review article, then maybe I could be competitive to get a job teaching law somewhere. The odds were long, she told me, cheerfully.

Bankruptcy is highly technical and not where a third-year law student should go for an easy A. The law is embedded in a statutory code, full of internal references. More confusingly, bankruptcy is about unwinding many of the regular rules of law. I had studied how to make contracts; bankruptcy was about how to break them. I had studied how to buy property; bankruptcy was about repossessing it. I had studied how corporate law incentivized risk-taking and allowed companies to raise capital; bankruptcy was about what happened when the bet was bad and the company was broke.

I found it all fascinating. As a teenager, when my dad worked at the bank, I would ride along with him to repossess cars. He'd drive the bank car back, and I'd drive the repo. For almost six months in high school, I drove a black Camaro and thought I was so lucky to have a cool car. I didn't think much about how unlucky the debtor was. In my farming community, everybody was shades of poor, and we all had our good years and bad years. In the 1980s and '90s, they were mostly bad. I never questioned the golden rule of American capitalism: The bank always wins.

In bankruptcy, the debtor could halt the collection calls and the foreclosures. They could keep some basic property, turn over anything above the allowed limit to pay off their creditors, and then discharge the rest of what they owed. The debtor got a fresh start. As Elizabeth explained, capitalism was inevitably going to have winners and losers. Bankruptcy was our economic and social response to failure.

Beginning in the mid-1990s and continuing while I was in law school, Congress considered major bankruptcy reform. The efforts escalated in 2000 as the presidential election approached. *Time* did a several-part story on the legislative battle, and reading Professor Warren's quotes in the article "Soaked by Congress" had inspired me to enroll in her class. Senator Chuck Grassley from Iowa was leading the charge to make bankruptcy less forgiving and less available to families. In the article, he admitted that his goal was "to make bankruptcy more embarrassing—and more difficult." As consumer bankruptcy filings reached a record high of one million per year, banks had convinced Democrats and Republicans alike that the stigma of bankruptcy was gone.

• • •

Shaking snow off my boots, I looked up and saw the lamp on, brightening the midafternoon dusk that is January in Cambridge. I trudged up the steps and stood in the doorway.

"How'd it go?" Professor Warren asked, jumping up and patting the couch for me to sit. "Tell me everything. This is so exciting."

I had come back from the bankruptcy courthouse in Boston, where I was conducting the first day of research for Warren's collaborative study, the Consumer Bankruptcy Project. Having earned an A, but not an A+ (to this day, Warren says my exam was excellent but not superb), I was doing an independent study course to assist with research into who filed bankruptcy and why. A four-page questionnaire asked people to volunteer information such as age, occupation, and reason for filing bankruptcy—all data that the courts themselves did not collect. Warren thought Congress was wrong that people were abusing the bankruptcy system. By surveying debtors, the Consumer Bankruptcy Project would produce hard numbers to show the hardships of unmanageable consumer debt.

I proudly showed Warren the twenty questionnaires I had collected. Flipping through them, I showed her that they were complete, and I reported that only one person had refused to participate.

"Excellent!" she said, clapping her hands. "Really great work, Katie. Now we can send you to Philadelphia and Chicago and eventually gather the thousands of surveys we need for a rigorous study."

I beamed and handed her the surveys.

"Did you have fun? Did you like it?" she asked, as I packed up my backpack.

"It was really interesting to see what we talked about in class happening in real life and watching people go through the process. It was kind of sad, though. Some people were really upset, or in wheelchairs, or had little kids with them, so I didn't bother them."

"WHAT?!?" Warren said, jumping up from her desk chair. "You didn't give the questionnaire to the sick old people?"

"No, of course not, because they had so much to worry about. Some people couldn't find their attorney, and there was this one baby that kept crying, and . . ."

"You messed it all up, Katie. You ruined the research."

"But how?" I pressed. "I got twenty questionnaires in only two hours. You said that would be a good response rate."

Warren sat back down. From behind her desk, she gave me a look that made clear I had failed to think and I had failed her.

"If you only ask the people who seem friendly or seem okay or seem healthy, the data will show only friendly, okay, healthy people in bankruptcy," she explained.

"But what if they are on oxygen, or blind, or speak Spanish?" I argued.

"Every single person," she repeated, to drive home the lesson. "If they give you a reason they cannot participate in the research, write it down on the declined survey. But you have to ask every single person. If you cannot do that, you cannot do the project."

I waited to respond, thinking that she would soften a bit, or at least acknowledge how difficult it was to approach people in a stressful situation and ask for their help by filling out a survey. She waited too, blinking once or twice as she stared me down.

"Okay, yes, I can do that, absolutely," I rambled. "Next time, I will ask every person who files bankruptcy to share their story."

At that, Warren pushed the completed surveys into her trash can. "Try it again, then."

I stomped home, dodging gray slush, back to my apartment from Warren's office. She was mean, I thought, not just to me but to the people in bankruptcy. How could she, sitting in her Harvard office, have any idea what it was like to have others know that you were broke?

• • •

When I was about eight years old, my mother did not have enough money at the four-aisle grocery store in Lorimor. Virgil, the elderly proprietor, was kind while I stayed with him at the register and listened to the uneven wooden floors creak under my mom's feet as she put food back on the shelves. I waited patiently and was a good kid, keeping an eye on my little brother and baby sister.

"Can we have Tootsie Pops?" I asked upon my mother's return.

They were our usual treat for behaving well on the trip into town for errands.

"We don't have any money. Put it down," she snapped.

I worried the whole way home and for months afterward how we could not have five cents for a Tootsie Pop. If we didn't have a nickel, we surely did not have a dollar. I have never told anyone about that moment, but I thought about it many times doing bankruptcy research.

In the next months, every time I gave out a bankruptcy survey, I hoped that I was not adding to the pain and fear people were experiencing. My shame at being broke was mostly private. These people, our potential research subjects, were literally "declaring" bankruptcy, and I watched them cringe when the bankruptcy trustee called their cases: "Martha Pontoski, Debtor #7382." "Hubert and Letitia Brown, Debtor #13-4432."

I traveled all over doing this work, and I remember that the only decoration in the big room in the Chicago bankruptcy court was a huge poster emblazoned with 18 UNITED STATES CODE 157, with fine print detailing the felony crime of bankruptcy fraud and its punishment of five years in prison or up to $250,000 in fines. I did wonder, then and now, at the irony of a big fine for people who were bankrupt, but the message was clear: Bankruptcy was not for cheaters.

In every court, the trustees generally kept things quick, verifying names, addresses, and signatures. People would start to explain their circumstances, but the trustees had full dockets and would cut them off. The trustee's job was to collect, but there were rarely any assets available to seize—with one exception in Philadelphia, where I watched a trustee take an engagement ring off a debtor's finger. The legal system didn't care why or how people got buried in debt, even as Congress assumed overspending and profligacy.

Most people wanted to answer our survey questions, especially to tell us in their own words about why they filed bankruptcy. Elizabeth Warren was correct: All kinds of people found themselves bankrupt and they all had long journeys to that low point. I started carrying extra paper because many stories spilled onto multiple pages, often starting with an illness or family change going back years. Part of my job was to type those stories into our database, and although the stories were so similar that none stands out to me, I think that was the very lesson to be learned. Financial distress did not happen to just my family; it happens to millions of Americans each year.

In 2001, job problems, health problems, and family problems were the causes of more than 90 percent of bankruptcies. Families addressed these challenges by borrowing, often accumulating tens of thousands of dollars in credit card debt, including fees and interest. After years of dunning letters and threatening phone calls, bankruptcy offered debt relief, so these families could focus on to-morrow's problems—often the same underlying job, illness, or family situations that prompted their borrowing in the first place.

Elizabeth was fighting to keep bankruptcy available to consumers against big banks determined to lend without restraint—and then collect without restrictions. I pushed her to study people in bankruptcy outside big cities like Los Angeles and Dallas, but she said that we needed to go where the most cases were to gather the data quickly. I wanted to study what happened to people *after* they filed bankruptcy. What's the point, she retorted, if Congress shuts down bankruptcy? She explained how each of the onerous rules would drive up the costs of bankruptcy and prevent people from getting help. It's death by a thousand paper cuts, she argued. By then, I realized how wrong I was to think that Professor Warren did not understand the pain of financial problems. She wanted the research done exactly right, surveying every single family, precisely because she cared so much about helping each one recover from financial ruin.

Eventually, in 2005, lenders like MBNA, Citicorp, and Ford Motor Credit changed the laws. It cost them over $40 million in political fundraising and many multiples of that in lobbying, in an effort that spanned fifteen years. As *The New York Times* astutely observed, "By definition, the critics of the [bankruptcy reform] legislation had limited lobbying resources." People struggling to keep couches and cars may have voted people into office, but they were not influencing how those politicians thought about their financial problems. Nobody was showing up at town halls sharing publicly how much they needed bankruptcy to help with their insurmountable debts.

But families had told me those stories in bankruptcy hearing rooms, and I had told Elizabeth and her other collaborators through our research, and those professors had told Congress and the American people in news articles, books, and TV appearances. In the end, despite the evidence, the banks got what they wanted. These new reforms slammed the door on many Americans, pre-

Elizabeth taught thousands of law students in an amazing career before Congress. I am her favorite, though, and I have this Medal of Excellence in Bankruptcy to prove it.

venting some from filing, and squeezing more money and heart-
ache out of those who made it to bankruptcy. It turned out that the
legal rules for bankruptcy were not as radical as I had thought initially in that law school classroom—the banks almost always win.

Elizabeth did not give up on helping families. She did not give up
on me either. I worked weekends and evenings while practicing law
to slowly advance my own research on rural families in bankruptcy
and on how families fare after bankruptcy, answering new research
questions. She cheered me on, pushing me to keep showing her
what I could do. And she did not hesitate to tell me to think better
and harder. My research let me escape from corporate law practice,
where I found little meaning, to academia, where my passion was
figuring out what the law meant in people's lives.

A few years into being a professor, after an academic conference,
I shared a cab to the airport with an eminent bankruptcy professor.
He was Elizabeth's peer, at a rival school.

"So, you are one of Elizabeth's students," he said. "I imagine that
she is a very *directive* mentor."

"True," I replied. "But she always pushes me in the right direction."

Asking her to be my mentor was a necessary first step. My life
changed with her guidance because I kept moving with her, continually trying to catch the hand she offered to pull me alongside.

13.

Personal Funds

When I ran for Congress, I was acutely aware of my short-comings: I was a Democrat in a Republican district, I had never whitened my teeth, I had not rescued anyone from a burning building or parachuted into combat, I had only worn a flag pin when dressed in costume as Sarah Palin, and worst of all, I hate apple pie.

My most serious failing as a candidate, however, was my purse. The ratty tote bags I used to haul kid stuff, and my faded backpack for lugging textbooks to campus, were cause for early rebranding of my look. ("Maybe just don't carry a bag" was my campaign manager's assessment of my personal style.) Upon election, I took the criticism to heart and purchased a lovely taupe leather purse qua briefcase, which I proudly carried for my first few months in Congress. But I soon grew tired of how heavy it was, how I'd lose my voting card in the multiple pockets that were advertised as a feature, and how my male colleagues carried nothing, free to glad-hand. The real problem, however, was what was inside my purse. Or rather, what was not inside: personal funds.

I first heard this phrase, "personal funds," in my orientation to Congress. There, we learned about the Members' Representational

Allowance, the money each congressperson is allocated to fund staff salaries and operational needs like postage and computers. We also learned that certain expenses couldn't be paid from these official funds; rather, they needed to be paid from personal funds.

For example, my travel to Washington, D.C., to be sworn in needed to be paid from personal funds or, if I wanted to go back to the fundraising slog only weeks after Election Day, from campaign funds. This confused me. I was definitely going to Washington in chilly January for work, not pleasure, and ethics guidelines strictly prohibit campaign activity in the U.S. Capitol. This was not an isolated quirk of the rules. Rent for offices in our congressional districts could be paid out of the Members' Representational Allowance, with no limit on how fancy or expensive the office could be other than competing budget needs. The security deposit required for any lease, however, had to be paid out of personal funds. My campaign could not give its mailing list of constituents to the Office of Representative Katie Porter for correspondence, but I could purchase these names for official use by paying with personal funds. Office equipment was to be purchased by official funds through approved vendors, but any lost or destroyed House equipment would be charged to personal funds.

I wondered what I needed to do to get these personal funds. Maybe I'd missed a required orientation event or failed to submit a form. I flipped back through the House Ethics Manual and searched the digital drive that the Committee on House Administration had set up. No dice. Finally, I turned to a fellow freshman colleague.

"Do you know how much we get in personal funds, for things like security deposits?" I asked.

He blinked several times.

"Ha, that's a good one," he laughed, slapping me on the back.

I had the sudden, terrifying realization that personal funds were, in fact, deeply personal. The policy of the House of Representatives, the so-called People's House, is that I have to use my family's budget to pay to serve the people. The same resources that I stretched to pay for my house and my kids' summer Scout camps were supposed to fund the $5,000 security deposit on my Irvine office. Congressional health insurance doesn't start on day one of the job but is delayed until February 1. This policy leaves members having to pay thousands of dollars from their personal funds for COBRA coverage, go uninsured, or cobble something else together. And if a staffer dumps their macchiato on their House computer, I would need to dip into my bank account to reimburse the House for a replacement, no different from when my daughter drops her iPad and needs a new one.

Other moments in congressional orientation revealed that I had not gotten a paying job so much as I'd ascended to a titled position. Three weeks after the federal government shut down in December 2018, the newly sworn-in freshmen congressmembers gathered to debate how to respond to federal workers going unpaid.

"We should not take our salaries," argued Representative Abigail Spanberger. "If workers are not getting paid, we are not getting paid."

The fervor grew, with other members expressing a desire to stand in solidarity with TSA agents, IRS employees, and other federal workers. I started to notice who advocated for refusing our pay: people with sufficient personal funds, whether from wealth or a spouse's income. I had no way to pay my mortgage or pay for childcare if I did not get my paycheck on February 1 for the first month I had worked. Federal workers were in the same boat, but sinking our own families into trouble wouldn't rescue them. The problem was the partisan stalemate that caused the shutdown.

"What are we supposed to do to make ends meet?" I asked. We were prohibited from getting second jobs, though I wryly noted that Congress distinguishes between income and capital not only in federal tax law, but also in its ethics rules: Stock dividends and business distributions were allowed, but wages were not. We wouldn't be eligible for food assistance or other help with bills if we were voluntarily forgoing pay. Representative Sharice Davids, also a single person without a spouse's pay, was plainspoken. "I'm broke," she stated, describing how she had quit her job to campaign (a luxury that I hadn't even had) and depleted her savings.

On our third day in Congress, the Democrats elected in 2018 glared at each other. The glow of unity in our shared new roles had faded. A majority wanted to refuse pay and demanded that we act in concert, in order to draw the most media attention. People who could easily skip a paycheck were shaming me for needing a paycheck. Their cause—advocating for workers—treated the very reason people work—the money—as a political prop.

They were oblivious to how the sacrifice of pay would be an act of class warfare of its own kind, evidence that politicians could afford to playact as workers, since the salary for most members was akin to an honorarium, not a paycheck. The title and role of congressmember was supposed to be compensation enough. I had signed up to serve my country, only to find that literal community service was the expectation.

• • •

The fundraiser was lovely and rather fun. White tablecloths and peach peonies adorned tables under a canopy, where donors listened to *Seinfeld* actor Jason Alexander. He had helped Democrats win in 2018 and was right back at it only a few months later, given that our next elections were in 2020.

"I'm here today with my beautiful wife, Daena," he gestured. "I love you, honey," he continued, "but if you ever leave me, I am running straight into the arms of Katie Porter."

I blushed but was flattered. Humor has always warded off insecurity and frustration in my life, and having to campaign for reelection only three months after winning office was bringing up all those emotions.

As the luncheon broke up, I was eager to get home. I had left my kids unsupervised, so I knew I would find a sink of soggy peanut butter and jelly sandwich crusts and an open bag of chips growing stale. I excused myself from a donor reminding me that Democrats need a new message (donors also need a new message, because I hear that complaint every day). Harley Rouda, who had just been elected to represent the neighboring district, put his hand out as I walked through the sleek monochromatic ecru living room of our donor's mansion.

"Could you have my car brought around too?" he inquired, thrusting a salmon valet parking ticket into my hand and turning back to his conversation. Shame and fury propelled me straight out the door and into the bright Orange County sunshine.

"What the hell!" I exclaimed, watching the dropping jaws and widening eyes of a handful of fundraising staff waiting to thank people as they left.

"Harley Rouda just gave me his valet ticket, like I work for him," I ranted. "I didn't valet my minivan. I parked on the street. Am I not in Congress, just as much as him? Did he not hear that I won my election too?"

A staffer grabbed Harley's ticket from me and headed to the valet attendant. My face flushed. As the valet navigated Harley's sleek Tesla past me, I climbed into my country blue minivan and headed down the hill, through the gates, toward home.

Harley loaned his campaign a cool quarter-million at many fundraising deadlines, totaling $1.6 million for the election. Given this, it burned me when Democratic leaders compared my fundraising unfavorably to his, suggesting that I needed to work harder.

Harley's self-funding was not unusual. The other Democrat who flipped an Orange County district in 2018 was a Powerball lottery winner who spent $8 million of his personal funds to win. Not content with being lucky and rich, Gil Cisneros went after the prestige of being a congressmember.

By this point in my life, I was used to rich people; I had cobbled together scholarships and part-time jobs to earn Ivy League degrees. But at Harvard, my straight-A grades equalized the economic disparities between me and my classmates. I figured, once I was elected, the work of being a representative should elide differences once more. As congressmembers, our titles were identical; our districts were constitutionally mandated to be identical in size; and our elections operated at the same breakneck pace of every two years.

But in the House of Representatives, the privilege of wealth divides ruthlessly. Ideological differences might be those most visible to the public, but the class differences cut the most sharply in our experiences. Gatherings like the Democratic Leadership Conference, President Biden's White House family picnic, and educational trips to a national park or a foreign country were, to me, all exciting prospects—and all out of reach because my personal funds could not cover the travel or childcare. I alternated between shame at my financial situation and resentment at how it isolated me. My experience as a House Democrat—in part—means accepting the painful hypocrisy of pretending to be equal, united by values of equality, when our lives were unequal, separated by wealth.

I could not help but compare myself to Harley. Within weeks of his election, he purchased a D.C. penthouse for millions. I rented an apartment for $1,600 a month that came with a mattress on the floor, no Wi-Fi, and cockroaches. Harley used his personal funds to purchase first-class upgrades on his flights, while I endured a year of flying to earn enough status to move forward from 33E to 9A. Harley combated the isolation and stress of the job by flying his wife to Washington, where she led the Democratic Spouses Forum. I raced to the airport to get home, both missing my kids and trying to cut my childcare costs. I spent a monthly average of $1,800 on childcare those first months, about one-fourth of my after-tax pay.

To be clear, the problem is neither Harley's existence nor his election. He ran and served for the right reasons, he loves our country, and he showed courage in casting tough votes. The problem is that Congress, and the ideals by which Americans measure our elected leaders, reproduce the class hierarchy that we claim to scorn. We want candidates with Bergdorf chic, despite our giving them a Target salary. Getting elected confers status, and in America, we assume that status comes with wealth. Voters confuse class and power, perceiving perks of salary, healthcare, retirement, housing, and travel that reality does not deliver.

Congressional salaries are $174,000. That pay has not increased since 2009; in real dollars, salaries are the lowest they've been since 1955. Our health insurance is purchased on the Affordable Care Act exchange. We pay 30% of the premium; the House of Representatives pays 70%, similar to most workplace insurance plans. I have a Kaiser HMO. Mandatory pensions take up 4.4% of the salary. Even with our gerontocracy, congressional pensions average $44,000 a year upon retirement. On top of that, two residences are required; votes keep House members in Washington, D.C., about a hundred days each year. No housing allowance or per diem is paid, and no tax deduction for business housing is permitted. And job insecurity is real; the average House member serves eight years.

Juxtapose these facts against the misconception that people become rich by serving in Congress. Bullshit. People often become congressmembers because they have the means—whether earned or inherited or through marriage—to disregard the pay, expenses, and job insecurity. Congress is full of multimillionaires for the same reason that the NBA is full of tall people. It's easier to get recruited and win with such advantages. Serving in Congress does not pad your bank account any more than playing basketball adds inches to your height. While we might accept physical attributes in athletes as natural or desirable, wealth does not give a better perspective for politics. It undercuts the purpose of representative democracy.

Americans rightfully fume that congressmembers trade stocks, convinced that insider information is misused, but we refuse to squarely address the harm that comes from representatives having such wealth in the first place. From 2019 to 2022, over 130 members of the House of Representatives each traded over $100,000 of stock. To trade that dollar volume in a year, these folks are either addicted day traders who cannot manage their money (much less our economy), or—and this is the reality—they own stocks worth many multiples of what they traded. Representatives who are my peers in age and years of political service—like Cindy Axne, Mike Garcia, Ashley Hinson, Ro Khanna, Tom Malinowski, Blake Moore, Kim Schrier, and Mikie Sherrill—have each traded over $1 million while in office. In my life before Congress, I knew that people with net worths in the tens of millions were not my peers. Pretending they are in Congress is an indignity.

Before he ran for office, Harley was a rich guy. In Congress, he ballooned into Representative Rich Guy. That transformation changed my occasional envy of him into institutional outrage. I ran for Congress to be a voice for minivan drivers and parents who silently lament $20 field trip fees. Once elected, I was tasked with fetching Teslas and leaving my own kids unattended in order to scrimp on my budget.

• • •

I am not rich, and I am not poor. I earned a good living as a law professor, enough to solely support my kids in a high-cost-of-living area like Orange County. My kids and I have enough food, a reliable car, health insurance, and enough devices to make screen time a constant fight. But like most households, money is a matter for consideration in nearly every decision we make. I have juggled 0% interest balance-transfer offers on credit cards on a couple of occasions, and calculated whether a tax refund would hit my account before the summer childcare bill came due. I have abandoned the $6.99 non-organic blueberries at the grocery store checkout and tried to assess the trustworthiness of the tire store guy saying that I cannot get another ten thousand miles out of my tread.

Budgeting, in the everyday sense of measuring the cost of each purchase or decision, is something I have to think about. Chase Bank CEO Jamie Dimon said he "would have to think about it" too—but only when I pressed him in a congressional hearing on how a teller at his bank could make ends meet. Using a whiteboard to break down the wages and costs of living, I switched to a red marker as the hypothetical single mother I was describing ran short paying for food and childcare.

"My question for you, Mr. Dimon, is how should she manage this budget shortfall while she is working full-time at your bank?"

"I don't know that all your numbers are accurate. That number is a . . . It is generally a starter job?" He chipped away at the question to avoid an answer.

"She is a starting employee. She has a six-year-old child. This is her first job."

"You can get those jobs out of high school, and she may have my job one day." He smiled smugly at this answer, hinting at the chimera of working from the very bottom to the pinnacle of an international conglomerate.

"She may, but Mr. Dimon, she doesn't have the ability right now to spend your $31 million [in salary]."

"I'm fully sympathetic," he said, cuing his lobbyists' preparation not to engage on issues of his salary.

"She's short $567. What would you suggest she do?" I pressed.

"I don't know; I'd have to think about it," he answered.

I asked whether the teller should borrow on her Chase credit card, or if she should overdraft her checking account, noting that the monthly budget did not even allow for clothing, medicine, or school lunches. Each time, he repeated that he would have to think about it.

As the exchange was replayed online millions of times, my colleagues asked me how I'd thought of this line of questioning. More than Mr. Dimon's refusal to acknowledge the mismatch between worker pay and household expenses, the wonder of my fellow representatives disheartened me. For all the bloviating about Democrats being "for the people" and Republicans advancing "a pro-worker agenda," I confounded politicians on both sides of the aisle by raising that exact topic.

Diversity in Congress means representatives with different experiences and identities: age, race, ethnicity, sexual orientation, gender identity, veteran status, and disability. With regard to money, however, the explicit and universal demand from voters is that congresspeople should all be "average" Americans. But implicitly and institutionally, the opposite is true. Both getting elected and serving in Congress almost demand a certain amount of wealth, a fact that voters prefer to overlook. The fawning memes of Nancy Pelosi exiting the White House in a terrific coat that she "found in her closet" omit the fact that it's a Max Mara design that cost $3,000.

Politicians are expected to be powerful and trusted leaders, yet we resent the fact that in our capitalist society, it's money that delivers the trappings of power and trust. Conversely, struggling with money is a cause of shame. Politicians should profess concern for poor people, but not actually be poor. The wealth of so many elected leaders reflects the beliefs that our economy and society inflict on us: doubt that poor people are competent; doubt that middle-class people are powerful enough to govern; and doubt that class is a fault line that deeply shapes decisions.

My bank account is better than average, and I thank my lucky stars to be in that situation. But I watch my checking account balance and not my stock portfolio. This puts me in a club with nearly all Americans. Congress puts me in a different, exclusive, elite membership, even if I cannot afford the apparent dues. My personal funds come from my paycheck, just like the people I represent. That's a strength, not a shortcoming.

14.

Bought Off

At Yale, I majored in American studies, which required courses in the literature, history, and social science of, you guessed it, America. (My dad said it sounded like something I could learn more cheaply by watching TV in our living room.) To graduate with honors, I needed to write a senior thesis, a long research paper for academic credit. Doing an independent study seemed better than waking up early for more classes and would give me an opportunity to do my own "ethnography." I would learn how my subjects explained their society, in the anthropological tradition of participant observation and fieldwork.

My dad's response to my scholastic pursuits was to spend the rest of my summer break exclaiming sarcastically about the number of job listings for anthropologists in the Sunday classifieds of *The Des Moines Register*—there were none. I reassured him that I could become a professor of anthropology, but that did not seem to assuage his fear that I would be living at home the next year after graduating with my fancy degree.

While he was not thrilled with whatever an ethnography was, my dad did suggest a feasible topic. The bank where he worked might open a branch in Princeton, Missouri, a small town where a corpo-

rate hog farm had rapidly expanded with $800 million in invest-
ment bank financing. A young guy from New Jersey, burned-out on
Wall Street, started the company to mass-produce pork in indoor
environments. "Pretty interesting," my dad told me. From him, that
was verbose praise.

So I returned to the farm, as they say, for my college research
project, examining how Premium Standard Farms, Inc., had helped
the town.

That summer, I interviewed a couple dozen people, from the local
librarian to the corporation's public relations director. Then the
third-largest pork producer in the United States, Premium Standard
Farms had come to Princeton after its residents successfully fought
off a hazardous waste dump. Most residents told me that it was better
to stick with the familiar stench of pig shit than risk being a dumping
ground for toxic chemicals hauled in from St. Louis. They described
a farming community being invigorated by corporate agriculture.

One of my interviews was with the town's only nonprofit, the
Community Action Partnership, an umbrella agency for social services. Inside the door, a young woman dressed in a green sweat suit
sat at a rickety card table covered with applications for food assistance and an advertisement for a free health clinic. I explained my
research, and she directed me behind a cardboard partition to her
boss, a stern-looking elderly lady.

I introduced myself by saying that I lived a few towns north, over
the state line in Iowa, and was doing research for college. I asked
how she felt about the corporate farm coming to town. She repeated
what I had heard from others. Premium Standard Farms was the
reason the town had added jobs, people, and services. The company
had paid to repave the sidewalks, donated to the school, put in new
streetlights, and even built a new restaurant (featuring, of course, its
own pork). The town's tax revenue had doubled, and Princeton was
the only growing community in two hundred square miles. Pre-

mium Standard Farms even made a "real nice Christmas donation last year" to the Community Action Partnership. I thanked her for sharing her thoughts.

As I left, the receptionist who had greeted me was standing near the door. She pressed something into my hand, and I paused to examine this unexpected gift. Suddenly, I was hustled out of the office and found myself back in the hot summer sun. Unfolding the paper, I read her note.

• • •

When I had left Iowa for boarding school, my departure sparked a rumor that Phillips Academy was a military school for pregnant girls, which I'm sure would have surprised its most famous alumnae, the two President George Bushes. From there, I went to Yale for college. With nine years of 4-H to burnish my authority, my experiences in rural America were fodder for my application essays. Admissions officers ate it up, with one reassuring me that their East Coast campus had squirrels so I would still be around animals, just like on the farm. I found that at fancy East Coast schools, being from a pig farm is almost considered cool. People tried to relate by offering that while they had never been anywhere near the Midwest, one time their Montessori preschool went to visit a petting zoo that had pigs.

To save money while in school, I flew home only at Christmas and was welcomed into friends' homes for shorter holidays. I was shocked to see that some people celebrated Thanksgiving with asparagus drizzled in single-origin olive oil, instead of canned green beans drowning in condensed cream-of-mushroom soup. I still serve the latter for family holidays because those crispy French-fried onions really improve a vegetable. But my time at elite schools taught me that beets and cauliflower were foods that city people actually wanted to eat. I could write an entire book whining about my hardships in adjusting to the cultural differences between my home community in Iowa and the Ivy League. But J. D. Vance's *Hillbilly Elegy* already does that, in the way that only a straight white dude who made millions in Silicon Valley could.

At Yale, I was a strong student and a strong personality (I suspect my colleagues would say these traits describe how I approach Congress too). I got a top work-study job tutoring gifted New Haven middle-school students in math, avoiding the humiliation of cleaning the cafeteria trays of my classmates. My best male friend took me to sold-out concerts in New York because his dad was president of Warner Music, and my freshman roommate taught me how to navigate the Upper East Side of Manhattan and even brave the crosstown city bus. Another roommate got us into the nicest dorm room, boasting a two-story suite with a private bathroom, perfect for hosting parties. I was outgoing and outspoken, edgy enough to be on the cusp of being a cool kid.

In the spring of my junior year, I was selected for Scroll and Key, one of Yale's secret societies. I would divulge more about that, but there were always rumors about assassins, and I have enough risk of bodily harm serving in Congress these days. Wearing a lacrosse sweatshirt (a sport never seen in Iowa), I zipped around campus from my honors classes to secret society dinners. I barely noticed the gargoyles that adorned Yale's Gothic buildings or paused to reflect on my privilege to be there. I was busy proving that my Iowa background was not going to limit my future.

Without any recognition that a few enrolled students were evidence to the contrary, my Yale courses on social prestige, income inequality, and class focused on the decline of the American dream. My favorite professor, an anthropologist, studied economic downturns and financial hardships. She guided us through books such as *Falling from Grace* and *The End of the Line,* and we discussed corporate downsizing, offshoring jobs, factory shutdowns, and declining prosperity for working Americans. The lesson was that corporations were good at making money and bad at helping people.

I got straight A's from that professor, but I could not square the idea that corporations discard workers with the fact that Fortune 500 companies were regularly on campus to hire. Management consulting and banking firms often came up from Manhattan to Yale, and I recall soothing myself when Booz Allen Hamilton did not invite me for a final interview with the fact that McKinsey & Co. would be more prestigious. I considered a management-track job at Procter & Gamble, but felt I'd be moving backward if I worked at the company's headquarters in Ohio after I had put in so much effort to get all the way from Iowa to Connecticut, the promised land of faux Tudor homes and country day schools.

Working for a big bank or consulting firm would pay enough to eliminate my student loans in only a few years, and I owed more than my dad made in a year. I didn't think a kid from Iowa could become a CEO like my friend's father, but he had thousands of people working for him, and I could be one of them. Unlike my family growing up, I could have a job with two weeks of vacation, a 401(k) retirement plan, a holiday bonus, and health insurance. I was proud of growing up on a family farm, but I was even more proud of being willing to leave when the only progress there was toward deeper poverty.

With the arrival of a big corporation, the town of Princeton, Missouri, seemed like a place to prove my professor wrong. Driving the hour south on the curvy blacktop road from my house in Iowa to Princeton to do my thesis research, the sights were markedly different from Connecticut suburbia. I stopped to snap pictures of weather-worn clapboard houses and roadside signs advertising eggs or chickens for sale. In Princeton, I photographed the abandoned brick storefronts of a former bank, variety store, and theater, alongside the new constructions of Premium Standard Farms: the corporate headquarters, the "pork showcase" restaurant, and the new Cedar Ridge Estates condominiums that the company had built to house workers. I never did convince Premium Standard Farms to let me inside the buildings where the company bred, birthed, fed, slaughtered, and processed 1.9 million hogs in 1995.

When my dad had told me Princeton wasn't like other small towns, I had imagined it was because of all the pigs. After visiting Princeton several times and not seeing a single hog, I realized he meant its energy of growth and rebirth. The local banker told me, "Now, we think there is a future. Now, we can spend a little money and make our property look better and take care of ourselves." From the new pickup trucks to the excitement that the nearest Pizza Hut was launching a delivery run from forty miles away, the town was bustling.

The corporation quickly became synonymous with the town. "We didn't used to exist as a community for so many people. They didn't know where Princeton was, and we didn't count for a lot in America," explained one person. They pointed to the framed articles in newspapers about Premium Standard Farms and how the corporation had funded the town's annual festival, saving it from extinction. The company affairs director ticked off employee and community engagement: the softball league, the holiday party, the game preserve for employees who hunted, and even the summer "pignics" that welcomed everyone in town, whether they were on the company payroll or not.

I documented these changes, writing in my draft about the importance of money to being able to participate in American culture. The farm economy had soured more than a decade ago, leaving rural Americans in towns like Princeton (and my hometown) worried about how to earn a living and provide a future for their children. Premium Standard Farms was putting money in people's pockets, creating an opportunity to live like other Americans.

• • •

When I unfolded that note from the Community Action Partnership receptionist, part of me wanted to throw it away. I was a college student in sandals and a T-shirt, not a spy. The note said there were others against Premium Standard Farms. Even if I had not been there long, how could I have missed such resistance in a town of 1,021 people?

I drove home, feeling like my research was failing, and fearing that my grade would too. Paying a decent wage and hosting a company picnic didn't seem like bribery to me. Premium Standard

Farms paid for what the town needed, and their corporate brochure declared: "Some companies start trends. We've started a revolution. A better company. A better process. A better pork product."

Better bacon definitely appealed to me. But a better company was the real attraction. My starting thesis had been that Premium Standard Farms was the savior of this small town, but maybe I was looking for what I wanted to find: a happy corporate ending.

I did more interviews. The school principal observed that there used to be one economic class in town—poor. Now he could pick out the kids whose parents worked for Premium Standard Farms because they had new clothes for the Christmas play.

Some people complained that Princeton was losing its independence and initiative and giving up on small farms. Others channeled populist concerns that "economic development" was just a buzz phrase; that the government was giving too many breaks and incentives to corporations; and that neighboring towns judged the people of Princeton for stooping to Big Agriculture. One farmer insisted that kids moving back to their hometown to work for Premium Standard Farms was a failure of capitalism, not a success. Those kids worked for hourly wages, for a CEO who wore a suit; but the farmer's definition of economic mobility was being able to own land and control your family farm's prospects. He told me: "It's the American dream to want your children to have a better life than you did. And having a job in those hog factories isn't better than the life that I had, and that's what everyone should want for their kids." I began to see the corporation's money as a corrupting and dividing influence.

In my final paper, I wrote how Princeton illustrated a "dilemma about economic social change." I softened from my initial optimism that Premium Standard Farms was rescuing the town, suggesting instead that the corporation offered a lifeline that only some people wanted. Others preferred to go down with their community, undisturbed by change. I concluded, "In a post-industrial global economy, all Americans need to be concerned about what types of changes our country will celebrate and encourage as progress." Lofty words, indeed, especially for someone who had not figured out how her own life should progress. There was celebration, though. My thesis won a prize, awarded at my graduation from Yale.

Two months later, Premium Standard Farms filed for bankruptcy, getting bought out by Morgan Stanley and Putnam Investments. Recapitalized and focused on boosting profits, the company cut its workforce and moved its headquarters from Princeton to Kansas City.

I was not sure then, and am not sure now, whether working for a big corporation amounts to being "bought off." (Politics certainly presents more daily peril of corruption than even investment banking.) But after spending time in Princeton, I quit competing with my classmates for interviews with corporate recruiters. I wasn't a farm kid anymore, but I was not signing up to be a creature of corporate America either. I didn't know what I wanted to do long-term, so I just decided what to do next.

I taught for a year at an international school in Hong Kong. I worked as a costumer for the Macy's Thanksgiving Day Parade. I took a solo trip around the world for six months. And then, like many college graduates without a better idea, I went to law school.

Places I've Lived

Little Rock, Arkansas
I clerked for a federal judge who memorably told young staffers to stay in their lane: "If you think I'm breaking the law, call 911 or the FBI. Otherwise, follow my directions."

Las Vegas, Nevada
Being a professor in Las Vegas is like being a sex worker in the Vatican: You're providing a valuable service to people who consider your profession irrelevant to the good life.

Kansas City, Missouri
Working as an intern at the U.S. Attorney's Office, I met my ex-husband at a martini bar. I only drink whiskey. Should've been a sign.

New York City, New York
As a costumer for the Macy's Thanksgiving Day Parade, I dressed Santa. My career thrills have been downhill since then.

Washington, D.C. (1st time)
As a Smithsonian Institution intern in its employee childcare center, the closest I got to valuable artifacts was keeping preschoolers from licking the protective glass.

Washington, D.C. (2nd time)
In 1995, I interned for Senator Chuck Grassley. His office responded to every constituent inquiry, an example that I now follow.

Out of a Backpack
Fifteen countries in a fifteen-pound backpack in fifteen weeks around the world.

15.

Unpacking

During my first campaign, people constantly asked me why I was running for Congress. Here is the answer:

I saw that our political system needed commonsense values. I was called to act, as so many other Americans before me, to serve our country. I was really concerned that the institutions that make this country great, like freedom and justice, are being taken for granted. We need elected officials who can find common ground and have the energy and passion to serve their community and country. I ran for Congress to deliver for the people, to lift up our values, to restore trust, and to get things done for our community.

If you didn't roll your eyes reading that paragraph, please do not open any emails asking you to wire money to Nigeria to save your third cousin who is being held hostage and needs a kidney transplant. That paragraph is pure bullshit, and if you didn't spot it, you're spending too much time nodding along to political hacks on cable news.

My "answer" above is fake, in the sense that I never said those things. It's real in that it is an amalgamation of actual statements that I found on my colleagues' websites under "Why I Am Running for Congress."

If it seems like jumbled nonsense written out on the page, imagine the person delivering it in front of a crowd, with some respectful but authoritative hand gestures, sporting a newly purchased flag pin on their lapel. Now it sounds a bit more convincing, right? That's why candidates get away with uttering these platitudes in living rooms around the country, right up until Election Day.

Candidates are not truthful when asked why they're running for Congress, but I think the problem is the question itself. It almost demands a lie, which should ideally mention God blessing America, freedom, democracy, our Founding Fathers, that children are our future, and the bald eagle. The truth is that every person *runs* for Congress for the same reason the chicken crosses the road: to get to the other side—to be elected to Congress. The correct question is: Why do you want to *be* in Congress?

I have two theories on why the correct question doesn't get asked. I presume that once upon a time, in a suburban community center, a candidate answered why they wanted to be in Congress with one of these honest responses:

- Because I am annoying my wife in my retirement

- Because I think I am better than the guy currently elected

- Because I am competitive and like to win

- Because I am tired of losing at golf

- Because I belong with powerful people

Elections were lost based on these statements, so political consultants reframed the question. They substituted the innocuous "run for Congress" version, which is distant enough from the end-game to prevent a candidate's naked response admitting they think being a congressmember will be cool.

My other theory is about all of us, as voters. Many of us fear that democracy is a sham. Our cynicism about politics inhibits us from believing Congress is a rewarding, productive place. If Congress is hopelessly and structurally dysfunctional, there is no convincing answer to why one would *want* to be part of such an institution.

Running for Congress, on the other hand, seems palatable to most people. After all, who doesn't like free appetizers and cheering crowds? Running for Congress is patriotic. Whereas actually wanting to *be* in Congress, well, that is either self-serving—or the ambition of someone naive enough to think that the government can be a force for good.

• • •

In 2012, when I worked for then attorney general Kamala Harris overseeing foreclosure help, I also got to cheer on Elizabeth Warren in her transformation from professor to senator. I became a literal card-carrying Democrat, brandishing my one-night credential to attend the Democratic National Convention in Charlotte, North Carolina. From the nosebleed seats in the arena, I listened to speeches, excited to know people who were on the national stage.

In the next few years, as Elizabeth became Senator Warren, and Kamala became Senator Harris, I stayed in touch with both women, as well as the staff who worked with them. In 2013 and 2014, I waited and worried through separation from my husband. On September 29, 2014, I was "returned to single status," in the words of the family court stipulation, which is just a gentler way to say that I was divorced. A month later, my ex-husband suddenly departed to live a thousand miles away in Portland, Oregon, and I realized just how single my status was. Every school pickup, every homework sign-off, every gallon of milk, and every dirty sock on the floor was suddenly mine and mine alone. The shared custody agreement that wiped out my bank account to negotiate was meaningless, and plans for alternate weekends turned into all-the-time parenting. I woke up every day grateful to be safe and happy with my kids, even if I was exhausted and overwhelmed by 7:00 P.M. every night.

During those years from 2014 to 2017, I sometimes wondered if I had lost more than a husband when my marriage ended. With nearly full responsibility for three young children, I felt like I couldn't handle any more challenges, and that I had to stay put as a professor at UC Irvine. It wasn't like I was doing nothing professionally. I developed and taught a new course on transition-to-practice for graduating law students. I wrote one hefty law textbook on bankruptcy law, and then another on consumer law.

But I longed for the careers that could have been, mourning that they were now impossible. I remembered standing in Harvard Yard in 2010, declining Elizabeth Warren's invitation to join her when she went to the Treasury Department. I pitched hard in 2011 and 2012 to get President Obama to remove the holdover Republican in charge of the bankruptcy system and appoint me, but to no avail. In 2014, I interviewed to be head of the Division of Consumer and Community Affairs at the Federal Reserve. I had never heard of the person who'd spent twenty years in the position, so clearly this job needed a go-getter, I thought, and I was going to get the job. I flew to Washington, D.C., for an interview as one of the finalists.

When I walked into the conference room and the interviewers came around to shake my hand, I made an unsettling observation. Every single person was wearing shoes that seemed to have come right out of an Eastern European pre–Cold War factory. Two women even wore actual pantyhose—the brown kind that I didn't know still existed. By contrast, I had purchased new open-toe kitten heel pumps, going so far as to paint my toenails red to set them off against the black patent leather. When they told me a few weeks later that I was "not the right fit" for the Federal Reserve, I couldn't really disagree.

When my next chance to work in government came, I did not make the same mistake. I watched as the 2016 primary unfolded, excited at Hillary Clinton's accomplishments in the Obama cabinet and Bernie Sanders standing up to corporate power. A few weeks before the November election, the Clinton folks asked me to join the transition team. I headed straight to Nordstrom and bought a full wardrobe of wool suit pieces, dark tights, and two pairs of heels in navy and black that the salesperson assured me could be described as "sensible." I packed it all in a big suitcase and bought a ticket to depart to Washington, D.C., the day after the election.

That morning, November 8, 2016, I took my kids with me to vote, explaining the significance of electing our first woman president. I dropped them off at school and drove to the grocery store, where I ordered a full sheet cake with HILLARY CLINTON written in bright blue frosting. I was ready to celebrate with 64-to-96 servings for my neighbors as I headed to our community center that evening to watch the election results.

Within an hour of my arriving at the celebration, despair set in. The men mostly went home to sleep it off, unsure how to console their wives. Nearly all the women drank too much wine, and many cried as the 2016 election was called for Donald Trump. The kids went wild because absolutely nobody was supervising the snack table. Children popped open sodas and scooped up piece after piece of cake, leaving behind only blue frosting stains on their lips as evidence. With an incoming President Trump, the adults knew that a one-night sugar rush was the least of our problems.

Hours past their bedtime, I tucked my kids in and then hefted the huge suitcase of fall professional clothes onto my bed. Through tears of disappointment, I took every one of those sensible new

We'd definitely been happier in the morning, when I took the
kids to watch me vote for the first woman president. This is
one of many times that I have been wrong as a parent.

items out, grateful that I had kept the tags on. Then, realizing that I
had to schlep everything back to the store, I put all the turtlenecks,
tights, and pantsuits back in the suitcase. A few days later, I confronted a very disappointed Nordstrom clerk.

"You want to return all of this? Nothing worked out?" she asked.

"Absolutely nothing," I said sadly, as I watched her scan each tag.
The long receipt of returns felt like a checklist of my disappoint-
ments about my future as a policymaker.

• • •

Unlike a shocking number of my Yale or Harvard classmates, I
never believed I was destined for the White House or a CEO suite.

All I wanted was to be a bureaucrat who made government help people. I dreamed of a windowless office on the third floor of some government building. I was devastated that I had lost opportunity after opportunity to toil away on exciting things, like the correct legal standard for student loan debt in bankruptcy or the rulemaking on the acceptable late fee for credit cards. Bureaucrats don't have the occupational prestige or heroic glamour of brain surgeons or fighter pilots, and I doubt any second grader has dressed up as a bureaucrat for Career Day. But it was all I ever wanted to be, and I had failed.

When Trump's election closed yet another door for me, I wasn't just sad. To be honest, I was bitter. I blamed myself and everyone else. I had sat out or lost out on multiple government opportunities during the Obama presidency. I was angry that my country continued to refuse the presidency to a woman, which, by extension, excluded a position for me. I castigated myself for not working harder at my own career and at helping to elect Hillary Clinton. I found little comfort in the idea of waiting four more years until Democrats would have another chance to defeat Donald Trump.

When I returned the clothes, I purchased a cheerful dress with a tropical floral print and purple-suede strappy high heels. My then boyfriend's brother was getting married five days after the election, and now that I was not going to be revising organizational charts for banking agencies in a makeshift cubicle in D.C., I had a different role: wedding date.

I owed him the date, as he had suffered a streak of sleepless nights because I had been crying myself to sleep in the days after the election. Like all sensible boyfriends, he wanted a girlfriend who didn't rebuff him in her gloom.

The bride had some Trump-supporting family members, and everyone was sternly warned to avoid politics to keep the peace. I behaved throughout the wedding, even smiling when necessary. A few people ventured to tell me that "it would all be okay." I was polite and refrained from telling them that they were fucking wrong. President Trump had explicitly promised a return to America's past, not a brighter future. As a single mom, an educated woman, a consumer protection attorney, and a professor of law, this presidency was not going to make things okay for me and those I loved.

After the wedding, with my purple heels in one hand and my boyfriend's hand in the other, I walked along the beach. I was tired of my own sadness and wondered whether I was being self-indulgent and self-pitying, or if I was simply being clear-eyed about the dangers that lay ahead for our country.

"I just wanted to make a difference," I wailed.

He stopped and put his hands on my shoulders.

"Katie, you do not need anyone's permission to make a difference."

"But I do. You don't understand; you don't get it. I will never get a position in Washington with President Trump in charge. All the policies that I worked on, they have no chance—and neither do I."

"Katie," he said more sternly. "You are the most impatient person that I know. Why would you wait for someone or something else? If you want to make law, then become a lawmaker. Just run for Congress."

My boyfriend told me that night about a girl he had known, whose then husband ran for Congress in 2006 and won election over an incumbent Republican. He had gone to a couple of early campaign events and described a low-key vibe, with the candidate talking with folks over beers and winning their votes.

"It didn't look that hard. If he can do it, you can do it."

He would rue those words many times over, through campaigns, impeachments, an insurrection, a pandemic, and three kids in puberty.

• • •

I told Tara, my longtime collaborator on protecting homeowners, that I was thinking of running for Congress. She said that I should do it.

I told my mom, who asked me why I was running for the House instead of the Senate. (My mom is a tough cookie.)

I told Michael Troncoso, who had been Kamala Harris's lead staffer on my foreclosure prevention work. *This is obviously the next right thing for you,* he said, pondering why he hadn't thought of it.

I told my college friend Tom Perriello, who had flipped a Republican seat in Virginia. *Decide if you care about winning,* he counseled. *Running is its own worthwhile experience.*

These friends introduced me to people who were coming off campaigns themselves. Folks like Erin Mincberg, who had fundraised for Kamala Harris in her 2016 Senate race, gave me incredible advice on how to be scrappy and frugal in setting up my campaign. Others emphasized avoiding unforced errors and focusing on building strategy behind the scenes.

On April 3, 2017, I declared my candidacy against incumbent Republican Mimi Walters. Day-one endorsements from Senators Elizabeth Warren and Kamala Harris immediately put the Republican establishment on notice about the race. Hillary Clinton had won the district, upending traditional Republican dominance in Orange County.

I started campaigning. I called the chair of the Orange County Democratic Party, I called local elected officials, and I called my first potential donors. That day, I heard the first doubts about whether I should run. I was too progressive. Walters was too formidable an opponent. I didn't have any experience in politics. There was another Democrat planning to run.

But it was too late—not because I had declared my candidacy; it's easy to drop out that early—but because I had made up my mind. I wanted to *be* in Congress. If Washington was not going to ask me to come, I would arrive anyway and on my own terms. If government would not be a force for good under President Trump, then someone needed to apply more force in the other direction.

In my past, I had never aspired to be elected. I didn't major in political science, serve in the military, lead in student government, or work my way up from local office. But I wanted to do the right things when I got to Washington, and it was this determination that launched my campaign. I was tired of people getting ripped off by corporations that cheated them, and a government that ignored them. And I was tired of not having any power to fix those things.

I decided to run for Congress to get power.

That is the naked truth about why everyone decides to run for Congress: They want power. The question we should be asking every candidate, every day, is what they will *do* with the power.

16.

Honest Stink

It was truly a cold day in hell. I had left my husband and toddler, Luke, at home because day care and most everything else was closed. I was stopped at an intersection, with the snow so heavy that I could not see the traffic light, when I got word to turn around. In a rare move, the University of Iowa College of Law had canceled classes.

Snow blanketed our yard with a fresh coat of white, and despite the dangerous roads and temperatures, I was grateful for the temporary peace it brought. Our doorbell had rung multiple times a day lately as volunteers canvassed our neighborhood for the 2008 presidential campaign. As the first state to pick a nominee, Iowa drew dozens of candidates and thousands of volunteers. A strong showing in the Iowa caucuses was seen as a boost to winning the White House.

My then husband, Matt, grew up in Oregon, where politics are decidedly more hands-off, given the statewide adoption of vote-by-mail in the 1990s. Matt viewed the presidential campaigns descending on Iowa as one of the best perks of living in the state. With each chime, he would race to the door. He saw the young canvassers from around the country—fumbling with campaign literature in bulky mittens, looking overstuffed in newly purchased winter coats—as brave soldiers in our democracy. Matt was genuinely flattered that these volunteers wanted to know his opinion on issues and would answer all his questions about the candidate they supported. "Tell me more," he would say, and the canvassers were delighted to oblige. Chatting with Matt offered a respite from having to ring the next doorbell in their fat canvass package of addresses. Matt was easy to persuade and a friendly soul, often offering a cup of hot cocoa for the road.

Meanwhile, I was juggling my job as a law professor and my role as a new mother, and I wanted my husband to close the door—and his mind if necessary—and focus on household responsibilities. I would fume at the canvassers wasting our time as I picked up building blocks, vacuumed up Cheerios, wiped down the high chair, and changed diaper after diaper. Matt was an involved father, but two-year-old Luke's interest in hearing, again, the board book about a dog named Spot could not compete with choosing the future president of the United States.

To be clear, I was a more committed Democrat than Matt, whose vote for George W. Bush in 2000 should have been an omen for our marriage's fate. Yet I had zero tolerance for the mania of the Democratic caucuses. While Matt raced to the door at each chime of the doorbell, I probably gave more due consideration to the teenager who stood on our doorstep selling magazines for their band trip.

Matt was weighing who to support in the caucus, while I was too exhausted after teaching all day and caring for a toddler to spend hours caucusing in a crowded gymnasium. I planned to save my political energy to vote in November for whatever Democrat survived to the general election.

Now, when I say that Matt was deciding which candidate he would support, I don't want to suggest any research on policies or careful consideration of experience or electability. He was more like a reverse Halloween trick-or-treater. To the canvassers, he was the mythical Iowa swing voter, and they were there to give him a treat to reward his role as a voter. For just a few minutes of his time and saying that he liked what he heard, Matt would be gifted with a big glossy yard sign, sporting a candidate's name and logo.

Matt would put the yard sign up for, say, Chris Dodd, and then for a few days while the sign stood, the canvassers would skip our house. The brick ranch at 1813 Liberty Lane was no longer "undecided, registered Democrat" but "lean Dodd" after they logged the sign in the canvass database.

Matt's mind would change precisely with the weather, and this was not a coincidence. While Iowa winters are the same length as winters everywhere, they are famously long because they feel that way. Ice, snow, slushy melt, and howling winds cycle through Iowa City every few days, and the winter of 2008 was particularly terrible. The sleet would dampen Chris Dodd's—or any other candidate's— yard sign (while Iowa voters were dampening his chances of becoming president). The wind would then blow it over, and inches of fresh snow would cover any trace of that campaign. Our house was once again home to the elusive undecided voter. The doorbell would chime again, and again, and again.

Between Thanksgiving and the caucuses in January, Matt was for Bill Richardson, Dennis Kucinich, Joe Biden, and Barack Obama. And those are just the dudes I can remember. He went back and forth with each door knock. His slogan seemed to be "The last one is the best one."

As the sun went down around four o'clock in the afternoon of January 3, Matt was reading numerous blog posts about how to caucus. Iowans crowd into a room, listen to instructions, and then hear their neighbors give speeches in support of their favored candidates. People then move to assigned corners of the room for an initial count. More speeches or cajoling follow as people change candidates based on the momentum and mood of the room. I was getting dinner ready, while Luke ran Thomas the Tank Engine trains off the edge of the coffee table.

"Should I make a sign?" Matt asked. "Do you think that would help make me more visible?"

Caucuses are like pep rallies, with supporters for candidates trying to build excitement and attract more Iowans to their corner. I ignored him.

"Aren't you excited? Being an Iowan is so cool. You're coming, right?" He was counting the minutes until he needed to leave.

I continued to ignore him, fastening a bib on Luke and serving up mashed potatoes and meatloaf, with an Elmo sippy cup of milk. I slumped into a dining chair and contemplated the tasks ahead: cleaning up from dinner, picking up toys, and the absolute worst—getting Luke to sleep. And then, I had to prepare to teach my classes at the law school tomorrow, while feeling overwhelmed that I had little time for research and writing.

"I'll stay here with Luke," I offered.

"But this is historic," Matt said. "Luke is an Iowan. We can take him to the caucus—Baby's First Caucus!"

This solidified my decision to skip the caucuses. Luke was too young to express his opinions on politics, but as his mother, I wanted to protect him. I had learned, long before I could vote, that politicians' relationship with Iowa was a one-way, dead-end street. As first in the nation in the primaries, we famously picked the president. But when the caucuses ended, all that the candidates left behind were soggy yard signs as spring thawed.

• • •

I am a born and bred Iowan. My brother, sister, and I shared the same bedroom that my grandfather and his four siblings had shared in the four-room white clapboard house outside Lorimor. My great-grandfather, Loda, built the home and a big barn made from walnut trees that he felled to clear land for farming. By the time I was a kid, the barn was starting to rot, becoming a spooky place inhabited by broken-down machinery and owls.

That farm was my childhood world, and I followed my dad and my granddad from task to task. I used a Sharpie to carefully mark numbers on ear tags for new calves, resolving never to get my ears pierced when I heard the calves bawl. When my grandfather bought a small but brand-new John Deere tractor, I'd ride behind him standing on the ball hitch while he went out to count cows. "Never

I wanted to grow up and be just like my granddad,
a farmer who wore Western shirts with mother-of-pearl snaps
and often chewed on a piece of clover.

ride in front of the wheel," my granddad would remind me. "Better you be muddy than you get flattened."

I never did fall off, but I took in every word of advice. I needed to learn all the rules for successful farming that Granddad and Dad knew because I worried whether there was a path for a girl to get out of the steaming kitchen, canning tomatoes and mashing potatoes, and into the air-conditioned cab of our biggest tractor.

In the late 1970s, being a good farmer meant being a bigger farmer. Agriculture was going global, with the Soviet Union negotiating a multiyear contract to buy grain from U.S. farmers. In 1973, President Nixon's secretary of agriculture, Earl Butz, called on American farmers to plant "fencerow to fencerow" and "get big or get out." Farmers bought more land and equipment, and our local banks were willing to lend. Decades after the hard feelings of the Great Depression, farmers and bankers were united in growing the agricultural economy.

Shortly after I was born, the farming boom allowed my dad to leave his job in Fort Dodge teaching community college. My dad sought to expand and modernize, using his degree in agricultural economics to buy and sell futures contracts for the pork we'd produce. In the early 1980s, he took out loans to add an aptly named confinement building to hold hundreds of weaned pigs being fattened up for slaughter, and we adopted no-till planting to prevent soil erosion and save time plowing hundreds of acres.

Farming wasn't easy, but Granddad and Dad loved it, so I did too. When a boy teased me in kindergarten that my dad smelled like hog manure, I came home in tears. My mom held me by the shoulders.

"You tell that boy, 'It's an honest stink.'"

My family was doing things right.

• • •

As a country kid, much of my childhood was spent on the school bus or waiting for it. My dad mowed a path in the weeds straight down a steep hill, so I could meet the bus where my mom could keep a watchful eye on me, rather than walking the quarter mile down the winding driveway.

The bus ride was over an hour, and I would read Nancy Drew or Laura Ingalls Wilder as we bumped along gravel roads. When that got old, I would stare out the window at rows of crops that changed with the seasons. In the winter, the trip was treacherous on unplowed roads; in the spring, thunderstorms would beat down on the roof of the bus. One day, we stopped at a nearby farm to pick up some kids, but all that was there was flattened metal and upturned trees. A tornado had hit their double-wide trailer the night before, and the bus just pulled slowly away. Rain made our corn and beans grow, but it could come with punishing storms that blew away homes.

I went to a consolidated school district, which was the result of a bunch of little towns being forced to share resources. East Union Community Schools covered half of the county, but that still meant only fifty kids in my grade when the three elementaries gathered at the high school in Afton for a district-wide assembly. As a fifth grader, I sat with the older kids in the back of the bus on the afternoon drive back toward the elementary.

At the end of an Iowa winter, gray slush filled the roadside ditches, but the roads were clear. We were rolling along when suddenly the bus stopped as we rounded the corner past the gas station. Afton wasn't much bigger than Lorimor, but it had an actual town square, with a little bandstand and playground in the middle and a few businesses on its four sides. Kids lurched forward and stood up to see why we were stopped. Pressed against the windows, all we could see were cars and pickups lining the streets around the square. Every parking spot was full. There was an honest-to-God traffic jam in Afton, Iowa, at 2:00 P.M. that afternoon.

We had a lot of experience being bored on school buses, but we had zero patience with traffic. Kids began to yell: "Let's go!" and "Drive, lady!"

Normally unflappable, the bus driver yelled back, "Sit down! Be quiet!"

That lasted about fifteen seconds, then someone asked again, "Come on, what's the problem?"

"The bank is closed," the driver said.

Some wiseass shouted back, "Duh, lady, the bank closes at noon every Friday."

That kid was right, of course. In the 1980s, small Midwestern banks closed for the day by midafternoon to process transactions before the close of business on the East Coast. And our local bank closed even earlier on Friday to catch up on the week's work.

The driver then said, "No, the bank is CLOSED."

In fifth grade, I didn't know what that meant. But the strain in the driver's voice was obvious to even the littlest kids on the bus. Something really bad was happening, and kids, too, were in harm's way.

The bus inched forward, and a crowd of people in front of Commercial Savings Bank came into view. That bank was the fanciest place I had seen as a kid, with its crystal chandelier and gold damask curtains. At that age, I had wondered admiringly how such a little town could be home to such an important institution. In front of the bank were four identical black sedans. These cars were not from around here; they were too new and shiny, free of dust from gravel roads. These were city cars, driven by people who wore ties, not caps given away by seed corn companies.

I fretted the whole way home. When I arrived, I went straight inside to look for my mom and then outside to look for my dad. What did it mean that the bank was closed? My parents shook their heads but didn't respond. That day was the first time that my dad and mom didn't answer a question I asked. And I asked a lot of questions—then and now.

I worried what the bank closing would mean for our farm and family. Even at that age, I knew we had bank loans. Coming home from selling our calves at the livestock auction, my grandfather would stop at the Afton bank to pay down our loan. When a tractor broke down, I would hear my dad debate trying to repair it versus borrowing to buy a newer model. If that bank, with its pillars and paved parking lot, could fail, surely our farm wasn't safe either. After all, we looked to the bank when we fell on hard times, to give us a loan to borrow at planting time. I was scared. Without a bank, who would bet on our future? How could we keep farming?

On Monday morning, the bank reopened. The black sedans had come from Kansas City, bringing federal regulators. They had closed on Friday to prevent a run on deposits and worked over the weekend to find a new owner to keep the bank afloat. The government backstop, the Federal Deposit Insurance Corporation, put in place after the bank failures of the Great Depression, worked. People who had money in the bank were safe. Our small bank was not important, but the banking *system* was. Our laws acted then (and still do today) to protect banks and their depositors from the risks of capitalism.

Years later, my mom revealed that she had not counted on government to stabilize the bank. When rumors had swirled a few days before it closed that the bank was in trouble, she withdrew our money. To keep it from burning in a fire, she stored the cash in a ziplock bag in our cavernous deep freezer, next to packages of white paper–wrapped hamburgers and roasts. I didn't know about the money at the time, and my parents were stoic, not seeing much point in talking about a global economy that they couldn't change.

The farm crisis had its origins in hifalutin economic policy: A grain embargo against the Soviet Union had destroyed demand, the Federal Reserve's "tight money policies" spiked interest rates, and farmland values plummeted as banks refused risk. But those things were thousands of miles away in Washington, D.C. I never saw them, and that is not what I remember.

I remember my mom's frown when she wrote checks, worried they might bounce. I remember my parents fighting about whether to apply for free school lunches for us or get in line for the infamous government cheese, the staple of 1980s food assistance. My mom took a new job fifty miles away in Des Moines, driving two hours to bring home a paycheck. My dad wanted to keep farming, but they both knew that farming was losing us money faster than my mom could earn it in the city.

A few months after it closed and reopened, my dad went to work in the bank. My grandfather had had a heart attack, and we couldn't afford any help to even try to keep farming. Instead of working outside in jeans and a cap, my dad wore a suit. He sat behind a walnut desk in an office, telling other farmers that the bank couldn't extend their loans. They could sell land at a loss or face foreclosure.

Some people did suffer their farms being sold at auction. Most were like us. They kept their house and a few fields, barely, but lost the way of life that they'd built. Equipment disappeared, barns went empty, and land was fallowed into the Conservation Reserve Program to hopefully reduce supply and boost commodity prices. Farmers blamed themselves for the farm crisis, and my dad was no exception.

In December 1985, a farmer walked into a small bank in Hills, Iowa, and shot the bank president dead. The farmer drove home and killed himself and his wife.

Would someone shoot my dad now that he worked at the bank?

Or would he shoot himself when he came home to a farm that would never feed his family again?

Neither happened, thankfully, but one tough year followed the next for farmers and rural Iowa. I saw that the contrast between the bank and our family farm was not just about interior decorating. Our bank was important enough to be saved by Washington, D.C., but our farms were not.

• • •

Two years after the closure, presidential hopefuls descended on Iowa. In eighth grade, I understood that farmers and small-town Iowa needed help from Washington, D.C. The farm crisis had lasted years; it was now 1987, and with this election, we could be done with that Hollywood actor, Ronald Reagan, and get someone who cared about Iowans and offered plans to help.

And it seemed like the candidates did want to talk to Iowans. Jesse Jackson put his national campaign headquarters in a small town only half an hour from our farm. The thirteen presidential candidates in competition on Caucus Day, February 8, 1988, together spent an estimated 846 days in Iowa, deploying 596 staffers to cover the state with their messages.

My parents, Democrats, and my grandparents, Republicans, debated who was the best candidate. I knew that my family had an important job to do in picking the president, especially with our first-in-the-nation caucuses. We had seen with our own eyes that Washington had policies to help our bank when it was on the brink of going under, and we wanted a plan to help us return to farming.

Yet, despite their antics at the Iowa State Fair and painstaking tours of all ninety-nine Iowa counties, the candidates sounded just like Washington insiders who failed to understand us. Most politicians offered macroeconomic jargon: "a support price geared to the cost of production plus a reasonable return," "incentive programs that curtail supply," "a negotiated worldwide reduction of barriers and subsidies," and "self-liquidating government loans." Both parties' eventual primary winners were somehow worse. Democrat Michael Dukakis suggested that Iowa farmers grow Belgian endive instead of corn and soybeans. When pressed on farm policy, Republican George H. Bush told farmers that he was "running for president, not secretary of agriculture."

Politicians in both parties seemed to agree: Iowa farmers had foolishly gotten swindled in a newly globalized economy. We needed to adjust to the risks and make better decisions. Nobody acknowledged that just a few years before, Washington had encouraged farmers to borrow and boost production, and that doing so was part of our Cold War strategy.

In November 1988, George H. Bush was easily elected. He chose a venture capitalist and former CEO as his secretary of agriculture.

• • •

When I was growing up in rural Iowa, canvassers never bothered to come to our farm. We were too few voters scattered over too many acres to make it worth anyone's time. As Iowans, it was our individual responsibility to get into town to hear the candidates and to caucus.

My childhood was mercifully free of doorbell rings and yard sign refuse, but it was full of the hardest lessons of politics. I learned that politicians cared about winning and that they dismissed as whining the concerns of farmers about how to feed their families and avoid foreclosure. Iowans were there to help politicians, politely listening to their promises in church basements and carefully considering

who to uplift as the leading presidential contender. But these powerful men were not there to help us, no matter how much we needed
them.

I knew two things about my future: I couldn't be a farmer, and I
wouldn't be a politician. If the honest stink of a farmer was not an
option for me, I sure didn't want the stench of politicians who failed
our farms.

17.

Talking Points

If I had a dollar for every time that someone told me the Democrats need a better message, I'd be able to donate the proceeds of this book, rather than counting on every penny to replace my nineteen-year-old dishwasher. All those people, whether they confront me in grocery stores or interrogate me on political TV shows, are correct. Democrats are bad at messaging.

While the competition is sad, I will nonetheless brag. I am good at messaging. Partly this is because I truly love to talk. When I see a person, I think, *Oooh, an audience for me.* Because I talk to strangers waiting in line and retail clerks in stores and literally anyone else I can corner, I am an experienced messenger of my personal thoughts. As a classroom teacher, I would talk for hours, with students having to wait for recognition from me in order to interrupt.

When I became a candidate, I knew I would need Strategy, with a capital *S,* to beat an entrenched Republican. I needed to find and follow the mythical "path to victory," which, it turns out, is just an estimate of how many people might vote for you based on analytics and polls. My contribution to winning would be my ability to talk, whether to regular people or the press. My plan was to delve into policy and tell people my beliefs. With that information, voters could make an informed choice and elect me over the Republican incumbent.

My first consultant was communications expert Nathan Click, who had the happy temperament of a golden retriever, combined with the killer instinct of a rottweiler. On the way to my early events, I would sit directly behind Nathan as he drove me in his sporty SUV. His surfboard occupied the front passenger seat and stretched into the back, and I'd frequently shove aside a wetsuit that I hoped was only damp and not moldy.

Nathan told me that my plan for engaging voters was nuts. I would not be telling people what I really thought about most things, and I certainly would *not* be explaining policy details. According to Nathan, my communication strategy was not to say anything that Republicans could use against me in TV advertisements.

"But that is not a message," I argued. "You are telling me my job is to not inform voters."

"Great, yes, right, uh-huh," Nathan replied. (For a communications person, he was remarkably imprecise in his own speech.)

"But I have to say something!" I wailed. "Voters are going to ask questions at events, and reporters are going to do stories."

"You need solid comms fundamentals," he instructed. "You need to learn the rules and stick to them. That way you won't lose."

I had naively thought that candidates were to single-mindedly focus on winning, but apparently "not losing" was the critical first step. From there, Nathan set out the fundamental rules of political communication for me.

"Write these down," he said, "and remind yourself before every event, every interview, every morning when you open your mouth to brush your teeth, that *this* is what comes out of your mouth. Don't just answer the questions. Stick to the rules."

Rule #1: Thou shalt use the buzz phrase

As President Biden delivered his 2022 State of the Union speech, my colleagues and I clapped on cue. But we also acted in tandem when the president broke a cardinal rule of messaging. The president explained that "immigration reform" is "the right thing to do; it's the economically smart thing to do." My friends, who had all been elected and reelected in tough races, intoned in response: "*comprehensive* immigration reform." We looked at each other and laughed. Like the dogs who were conditioned by Pavlov, Democrats are drilled to use that buzz phrase.

When Nathan told me to answer any related question with enthusiastic support for comprehensive immigration reform, I pointed out that President Trump engaged in comprehensive immigration reform—by building a wall and putting kids in cages. Clearly, that phrase could mean anything.

"Yes, right," said Nathan. "Now you are getting the idea. People are so divided, and you'll just get into trouble."

This same thing happened with "healthcare is a human right." I pressed on what exactly that meant for patients, providers, costs, and quality. People need to know how it will help them, I argued to Nathan. I knew firsthand that a patient cannot win an argument with an insurance company by saying that "healthcare is a human right."

"True," said Nathan, "but you are not a policymaker yet; you are a baby candidate, and the Republicans are going to trip you up. Say 'healthcare is a human right,' and nod your head sympathetically. When you get to Congress, you can yell at Big Pharma and private equity companies buying up safety-net hospitals."

I miserably took Nathan's advice during the campaign, then joyfully took his offer to let loose on corporate greed in healthcare when I got to Congress.

Rule #2: Thou shalt honor the interviewer

When she moved from professor to candidate, Elizabeth Warren told me that she struggled to realize reporters were not students. In a classroom, if someone is not seeing your point, you try a different angle, sharpen the example, and pound the lesson. With reporters, you grit your teeth into a smile and give the same answer. They may ratchet up and be more aggressive, but the rule is to rinse and repeat your answer (preferably with a buzz phrase, per Rule #1, above).

What you definitely do *not* do is mix it up and confuse an interview with a heated holiday-dinner-table discussion with your eccentric relatives. The rule is to honor the interviewer. Praise the question by saying, "Thank you for asking." Do not interrupt, do not argue, and definitely do not say they are stupid.

Given how poorly I took Nathan's lessons on "good" media fundamentals, I am amazingly still friends with him. In my first year in Congress, I was a guest on the show *Real Time with Bill Maher*. Nathan had long since moved on to other campaigns, but I invited him to watch me in the live studio audience. I had gone from speaking to a half dozen people in a living room to late-night HBO, and I was eager to show off my media mastery to Nathan.

Two other guests, Charles Blow and Clint Watts, joined me on the panel with Bill Maher. They bantered back and forth, drawing laughs from the audience. I just sat there, feeling like a feminine decoration to be seen and not heard. Complaining per usual that Democrats are too liberal, Bill explained that he had always been "squishy" on abortion because his mother was told by her doctor that having him could endanger her health.

Unable to help myself, I broke Rule #2. A man explaining pregnancy to me—I'd had two difficult births (and one easy C-section)—was going to be set straight.

"Well, Bill, I think that is exactly the point. Your mother made her choice." I stared at him, then turned to the camera and gestured with a smile to the audience. "And we are all here, living with the consequences of that choice."

The audience roared. Bill stood up, pointed his finger at the audience, and said, "Fuck you, fuck you, and fuck you." He sat down, looking a little shaken, and changed the topic.

Nathan met me backstage afterward, and I braced myself.

"I'm so, so sorry," I said.

"That was so great," he said, grinning. "You can't teach that kind of messaging genius."

The rules might keep you from losing, but big victories sometimes require breaking them.

Rule #3: Thou shalt respect the voters

At least in the early days of my 2018 campaign, I generally took Nathan's advice. I was frustrated that this man-child was in charge of every word that came out of my mouth, but he frightened me with the risk of a million-dollar mistake that would arm Republicans with an attack ad to sink my campaign.

"What should I say if I really don't know, and don't have a stupid buzz phrase?" I asked Nathan.

"Go back to your voters. You are running for an elected office. Make it about them."

Following this conversation, Nathan produced his best work product: the Safe Zones. If you are unsure what to say, start with these phrases, he instructed, to cue you to think about voters:

- When I talk to people here in this district, they tell me . . .

- This is another example of how our leaders in Washington aren't working for our families . . .

- Orange County families are fed up with what they see in Washington . . .

- There are a lot of misconceptions about families in this district . . .

These prompts all show respect for voters. And when I broke this rule, I went for broke.

A few months into the pandemic, I was trapped at home with my three kids when the temperature spiked. Without air-conditioning, our house was unbearable. My neighbors had air conditioners that rumbled like jet thrusters, so it was too loud outside. To find a place for an interview with *Desus & Mero* on Showtime, I retreated to my quiet place: the minivan. It made for an odd setting, but the hosts were car junkies and loved it. We reviewed the color (country blue), the model (Sienna), and the number of cup holders (seventeen!).

Then they asked whether driving a minivan lost me credibility in bourgeois Orange County. In that moment, I loved my van—and its air-conditioning and quiet—so much. Bringing the protective energy of a single mom, I gave what was charitably characterized later as a "hot take."

"They look down on me 'cause I drive the van. Then, those bitches want to borrow my van 'cause none of that shit fits in the Escalade."

As a large carpool vehicle for Scouts, and as a hauler for oversized purchases, my minivan was very popular in my neighborhood. But when I had to valet the van at a restaurant, the moms gathering for a late lunch of salads (no cheese or croutons, please) after Pilates looked at my Toyota Sienna with pity in their eyes.

My minivan has vanity license plates that read OVRSITE.
With this attitude, I do a full stop, not a California roll, at intersections.

After I said it, I knew I had spoken ill of constituents, breaking the rule. In a tough area like Orange County, you cannot afford to throw away the Cadillac Escalade vote.

Rule #4: Thou shalt be unflappable

Adhering to the political messaging rules requires poise and discipline. As the early months of the pandemic ramped up Congress's workload in the spring of 2020, I was lacking both qualities. I could barely figure out how to watch my three kids, let alone work even harder.

I left my kids to their own devices (literally to their phones and tablets) for a few hours and rushed into my Irvine office for a conference call with other congressmembers. When I got there, the phone rang, with my scheduler asking if I had forgotten that I had a Zoom interview with Samantha Bee on her show, *Full Frontal*. I had not prepared either physically or mentally. But I quickly logged on, the camera pointing straight up my nose in the institutional office lighting.

Sam asked her first question. "Are you exhausted from appearing in every Republican's nightmares?"

I said exactly what I thought, letting my mood show in delivering the answer: "No, I think that's a very comfortable role for me. If you're full of bullshit, I'm coming for you. Like, I just don't have time. I'm a single mom. Dinner's burning. I'm late to something. I have four thousand emails. My hair's frizzy. I haven't shaved my legs in a week. No. Bull. Shit."

Far from the unflappable candidate, I had channeled every parent's pandemic juggle into a ten-second rant. The clip was viewed 2.5 million times in the first few days after it aired.

Rule #5: Thou shalt not "no comment"

Given all the ways things can go wrong, saying nothing seemed safe—or so I thought. Rushing to vote one day, I was flagged down by a reporter in the gaggle, who blocked my entrance to the House floor.

"Representative Porter, what do you think about the effort to recall California Governor Gavin Newsom?"

Not wanting to be rude and ignore the question, I responded, "No comment." The ethics rules prohibit any campaign activity on federal property, and Gavin was a Democrat facing an election.

A few hours later, Nathan called. The *San Francisco Chronicle* had identified me as a "notable exception" to the Democratic support for Newsom, noting my refusal to comment when asked about helping Newsom or what Democrats should be doing ahead of the recall. The governor and his team were unhappy, understandably, as

I had endorsed him. I tried to explain that I was just following the rules of House ethics.

"You cannot say 'no comment,'" Nathan explained. "That is answering that you are uncomfortable answering."

Ugh, I thought. Political communication should be more sophisticated than the maxim we teach our kids: *If you don't have anything nice to say, don't say anything at all.* That is the rule, Nathan explained. I still had a lot to learn to stay out of trouble.

• • •

If a candidate follows all these messaging rules, there is one guarantee: The candidate will not have a meaningful message. But there is an important corollary: The candidate will not lose because they said something stupid—mostly because they will not have said anything at all. Word salad may not taste delicious, but it can never be poisonous.

I followed the rules in my first campaign in 2018. My messaging was "solid," also known as lame. As a result, I did not lose. The win, however, was delivered by everything except my communication efforts: door knocking, TV commercials, and a Republican incumbent who underestimated me.

When I arrived in Congress, everyone pretty much ignored me for the first couple of months. I had no opportunity to say anything wrong because I was not talking—not even to strangers. I was lost in the Capitol basement between meetings, trapped on flights and connecting flights and return flights, and sitting in meetings trying to figure out what people wanted from me.

When I started to speak up, congressional hearings were my venue. Limited to five minutes of responses from CEOs and top regulators, I had the backstop of stern and strong Chairwoman Maxine Waters gaveling me down if I managed to make financial services too entertaining. My words, especially the ones I wrote on a whiteboard, got attention and built my reputation as being willing to ask hard, honest questions.

In the press, at public events, and in town halls, I stuck to talking points. My new messaging maven, Jordan Wong, like Nathan, gave pointers and feedback if I strayed. He wrote speeches that I'd give on the House floor and crafted bullet point after bullet point of sound messaging guidance. I can read, even when I am tired and frustrated, and I aimed those bullets and fired them off.

But the physical lockdown of the pandemic set me free of messaging confines. Doing interviews without a staffer to help, I had other concerns: My overhead kitchen lights gave me a halo; the video-call link didn't connect; my kids would walk into my shot. I had no capacity for saying anything except exactly what I thought. In those early days of COVID-19, when bodies piled up in freezer trucks outside of New York City hospitals, the relative harm of a Republican attack receded. If these were my last days on Earth, I was going to spend them speaking honestly.

I broke rule after rule, and incredibly, I lived to see the next day. I talked about coping with lockdown by switching to "stretchy pandemic bras" and revealed that my home office was just my kitchen. I vented that people were acquiring and naming sourdough starters and learning how to turn salami into roses for at-home charcuterie plates, while I had simply started serving cereal twice a day to deal with the end of school lunches. Roaming my street while giving an interview, because it was quieter than the video games inside, I asked a reporter to hang on because I stepped in dog poo. I then lamented that my congressional colleagues would never admit that they had ever—in their whole lives—stepped in dog poo, when we have *all* had that unsavory experience. The journalist printed that in *Elle* magazine. I am quite certain I am the first person to talk about wading into actual shit in a fashion magazine, and I still got re-elected. Huzzah!

I told America who I really was and what I really thought. The result was that being Everywoman was described as my superpower. Now, at least most of the time, I am not afraid to communicate my thoughts, to share experiences, and to tell the truth.

If I am frustrated that Senator Joe Manchin is tanking efforts to make childcare affordable, I say that he is hurting families. When health insurance companies take premiums and deny care, I call it what it is: stealing. The oil pipeline disaster in Huntington Beach, California, was not an accidental "spill" like milk from a kid's cup; it was a leak and it spewed contaminants into the ocean. I will not say that COVID-19 has "impacted" us. The disease has not made an indentation; it has brought grief and death and fear, and we should use those words to describe its harms.

Republicans do have it easier with messaging. Their core message is that government is bad. When they use jargon or spew mumbo jumbo, the fact that such language makes them seem slimy and untrustworthy just reinforces their point—government cannot be trusted to be truthful. In hearing them, you are reminded of the fact that politicians are sus, and given that, you better vote for the guys who don't believe in government.

Better Democratic messaging will not be born out of a trio of repetition that we are fighting for "children, children, children"; an alliterative slogan like Build Back Better; or trying to reboot the U.S. Constitution by adding a hashtag like #ForThePeople.

If Democrats want Americans to trust us as leaders, we have to trust people as voters. The touchstone of effective messaging is simply wanting to be understood. Whether I am persuading voters or yelling at my kids, I don't leave any room for interpretation. Take or leave me, but know me.

Jobs I Want After Congress

When we're still voting on the House floor after midnight, I start planning my future career. These daydreams are also security blankets when polls show me losing reelection.

Radio talk show host:
You've heard the expression "a face for radio"? Well, I have an ass for radio. I could fill hours of airtime with spicy, thoughtful content — so long as I could wear yoga pants.

IRS commissioner:
Even the Bible spurns tax collectors, but if death and taxes are inevitable, we might as well do taxes right. Bezos, get ready to pay up!

Skort designer:

Stretchy, practical, and modest, skorts are perfect for minivan driving. But middle-aged ladies should not be limited to navy blue, black, or—worst of all—white. Can I get a periwinkle or a floral print?

Succulent landscaper:

When my daughter wants my attention, she yells "Succulents!" because I love them. My only hobby is making succulent arrangements.

8th grade math teacher:

In my real first job, I invented lessons like Musical Monomials. I could bliss out to the aromatherapy of Expo markers <u>and</u> train a future generation of whiteboard warriors.

18.

Correct the Rumors

My experience in politics is more *Veep* than *House of Cards*. One of the only fights that I had with my first campaign manager, Erica Kwiatkowski, was over whether I could stand on a stool when I was addressing crowds. I wanted people to see me; she felt our raggedy campaign was already too close to a comedy to invite further comparisons to Julia Louis-Dreyfus playing a vice president who used a stool to see over the podium.

But *House of Cards* does reveal a political character that is all too real: the "oppo guy." Mine was named Ace Smith. He's been compared to Michael Corleone in *The Godfather*, a soft-spoken, ruthless character who knows how to insert the knife. He was an early hire; everyone said he was the best, but we didn't speak in the entire first year of my campaign.

In March 2018, a few months before the primary election in my first run for Congress, a tweet appeared from a seemingly random guy, Kevin Matthews, in response to a post about the Republican incumbent congresswoman. The tweet doubted that I could beat her and discouraged people from voting for me.

California has open primaries, in which candidates of all parties are listed on the same ballot, with the top two vote-getters advanc-

Even Paul giving Betsy bunny ears, and a way-too-small
stool, cannot taint the sweetness of my first victory
speech, for the June 2018 primary election.

ing to the November general election. One winner would be Republican Mimi Walters, who had won reelection by 17 points in 2016. I was competing for the other spot against four Democratic men: Brian, Kia, Ron, and Dave. I had lost the California Democratic Party endorsement to Dave Min a few weeks before.

The tweet prompted my first encounter with Ace. His time was valuable, more than mine apparently, so I flew to San Francisco to his office. In a cramped conference room, Ace told me that my own life could doom my campaign. He gestured at the hundreds of pages of court files that I had overnighted to him.

"You are a domestic abuser. You put your kids in danger," he said. "This is bad."

"Those things are not true," I explained. "That is not what happened."

"It says those things right here. You'll lose votes; you could lose the election because of it," Ace charged.

"The judge, the custody evaluation, and the police all believed me. Those things are not true," I insisted.

He said just three words back: "Restraining Order Porter."

Ace stuck a knife in me—his own client—with those words, repeating what Kevin Matthews's tweet had said: "I doubt Katie 'Restraining Order' Porter could get it done" and beat Mimi Walters in November.

Through tears, I heard Ace's colleague, Sean Clegg, explain that Ace was simply saying to me what an opponent could, and likely would, say to try to win. It didn't matter if the allegations were true. It mattered that someone could cut and paste and edit and omit and come up with the damaging picture that Ace was painting.

A master of opposition research to discredit his client's opponents, Ace also knew how to defend against dirty tactics. His solution was strategic and savvy. But it is the only thing that I've done in politics that I'm ashamed of—telling the truth about how my marriage ended.

• • •

A few weeks later, I told my story to Laura Bassett, a reporter for *The Huffington Post*. She was patient with me, giving me time to explain and answer her questions. At Ace's suggestion, we were getting ahead of possible hit pieces that built off the tweet referencing my divorce. The idea was to describe what happened in my marriage and divorce in my own words, from my perspective, and that by doing so, we would curb the ability of my opponents to surprise voters with any allegations about domestic violence.

These tactics, and the words that describe them ("getting ahead of it," "controlling the narrative," "pitching your angle," and "shaping the message"), have negative connotations and real consequences. People often assume politicians compromise their values and seek to get ahead at all costs. When I shared my story of domestic violence, I did both those things. I compromised my values and I got ahead at a very high cost.

To be clear, I told the truth. I did not omit anything, I answered every question, and I backed up everything with hard evidence. The subsequent *Huffington Post* story described the abusive acts of my then husband and my calls to the police for help in 2013. After he punched a hole in the wall next to where I stood, he was arrested and jailed. The police had an emergency protective order issued; the next day, I filed for a restraining order to keep the kids and me safe.

A week later, minutes before the hearing, my husband filed a motion seeking a reciprocal restraining order against me. The judge denied not only his motion but mine, a clear violation of California law, given the evidence to support my motion: a police report containing my husband's own admissions of violence, photographs, and my statements under oath.

My lawyer told me that I needed to leave my house with my three children—then ages seven, four, and one—in the next few hours, before the emergency protective order expired. I squeezed my daughter's high chair into the back of my minivan, along with her diaper bag and a few books for the older boys. I packed one big suitcase, tossing in sippy cups and plastic dishware among T-shirts and shorts. We drove to a rental unit that I had located an hour before. I told my children it was a vacation, credible as it was a furnished vacation rental. I set up Betsy's portable crib next to me, and the boys shared the other bedroom, with a little bath in between. Nobody knew our address, not even my parents or my lawyer.

We lived there for a month. I kept the kids out of school at first, afraid that my husband would pick them up. The court had issued no custody order and given no guidance, but because of the police report, an evaluator from the Department of Children and Family

Services visited our temporary home. She ran through a checklist of questions on how I cared for the kids each day. Then she asked questions about how I was coping with recent events. That part made me want to scream. How could I not be angry, upset, heart-broken, and scared? The investigator did not care about my feelings. The only question was whether I was providing a safe environment for the children, so any hostile expression from me was risky.

Eventually, our lawyers reached an agreement. My husband would complete counseling, have phased-in supervised visitation, and eventually we would share custody pending a full custodial evaluation. Months later, the report recommended 70 percent custody to me and 30 percent to him. We settled on that arrangement, but within a month he moved to Oregon, leaving me with full responsibility for our kids.

When I ran for office four years later, I expected questions about being a single parent and about how I would do a demanding job with three young children. But I was unprepared for the possibility that my decision to get help to keep myself and my kids safe would be used as a political weapon, that my actions as a wife and a mother protecting her family would be seen as disqualifying. I dug through social media and public records to uncover the fact that the author of the tweet demeaning my restraining order had donated thousands of dollars to Dave Min's campaign. Kevin Matthews lived three states over in Denver, and social media had pictures of Dave and his wife with Kevin and his spouse. It was a near certainty that my opponent had shared details of my divorce.

My other primary opponents told me that Min had told people about the restraining order, that my kids were messed up because of it, and that I had "character issues" that made me unelectable. I had heard rumors of this narrative but had chalked them up to my being a single mom.

The *Huffington Post* story followed Ace's talking points. I was defiant about being accused of wrongdoing, when what I did was get help as my marriage ended in violence: "What happens here matters, because voters around the country are gonna see—does this mean you can't run for office, because you've been hurt or a victim? I think it's really important to stand up for that. We don't silence victims and we don't silence women for having experiences that are frankly all too common among us."

Following the story's publication, my campaign settled back into its rhythm. I raised money, I knocked doors, and I recruited volunteers. Dave Min sent out negative mailers about me, accusing me of having falsely claimed to be a lawyer, when I was licensed to practice in Oregon, not California. He accused me of having a campaign funded by special interest money, apparently referencing End Citizens United, a group that ironically works to end the influence of dark money in politics. He said not a word about my divorce or experience with domestic violence. Not a single voter expressed concern, although some shared similar stories about themselves or daughters or sisters. I was relieved to have moved past the shadow cast by my ex-husband's past violence.

In June, I won the primary. My campaign had turned the opposition's research on its head, making a potential weakness into a strength.

I regret that so much. I would take it back if I could. Because in the months that followed, my children learned the details of the story. Some volunteers told them that I was brave to leave their dad. The internet took care of the rest. The younger two children didn't remember anything, and my eldest only wanted to forget. My ex-husband was frustrated and upset, feeling that even after moving to Oregon and allowing years to pass, he could not move on. He complained to the kids of the unfairness of not getting to tell his side of the story. Luke furiously told me that I had no right to share private things about his life. Paul questioned whether the police had made his dad move thousands of miles away. Betsy begged me to stop being "mean to Daddy."

When my daughter learned that I was writing this book, she pulled out her sparkle unicorn notebook and a fat Sharpie. She had some ideas:

After discerning that "Navado" referred to the fact that Betsy had just learned I had taught for a year at the University of Nevada, Las Vegas, I asked what rumors I was supposed to correct.

"The stuff about my dad," she said. "You can tell people the story isn't true."

I gently explained that it was true.

"But you didn't have to tell everybody," she said.

I had heard this before from Luke and Paul.

"Betsy, it wouldn't be fair if I had lost because I got a divorce. I didn't do anything wrong."

"But it was wrong to tell everyone," she insisted. "And now you are going to do it all over again in this book."

And I have. Again, I question whether I am compromising too much as a parent for the sake of my public life, telling my story to help others even when I know it will hurt my children.

Being a real person and having a real life is in fundamental conflict with American politics. There is no way that I could've kept my privacy about the domestic violence in my family and gotten elected. There were real costs to telling my story, and even as I pretended otherwise, I knew that I was making a choice between my kids and my campaign.

• • •

A few months after I was elected to Congress, Speaker Pelosi invited me to a press conference following the House's vote to renew the Violence Against Women Act. Because of the *Huffington Post* story, I was invited to give one minute of remarks, along with a lineup of a dozen other congressmembers.

My communications director, Jordan, had written a short statement about my personal experience with a badly trained cop who responded to a 911 call when my husband was violent. The officer explained that I "needed to figure out a way to get along with my husband," and told me that if I called for help again, the police would take the kids to Orangewood children's home, the local juvenile facility. I had a full-blown panic attack when he said this, terrified at the idea of losing my children.

As a result, I didn't call for weeks. My ex-husband got angrier and more violent, as the realization that we were divorcing became clearer. I slept with a chair propped against the doorknob in the guest bedroom. When I called 911 the second time, after my husband put his fist through our bathroom wall, the officer who interviewed me followed every best practice. He reinforced that I was safe, that I had options, and that it was important to report crime. He had been trained to take statements from victims and from children and knew what the law required in domestic violence situations.

When I told the story and got to the part about the risk of losing my kids, I couldn't stop my voice from cracking and my eyes from shedding tears. My colleagues stood behind me as I described how the police officer training that the Violence Against Women Act authorized had mattered in my life.

"I'm sorry," I said to my colleagues, as I shakily took a few breaths to let me continue my remarks. Then Representative Karen Bass gave me a hug and told me that I had nothing to be sorry for, that my speaking was important in that moment.

I was willing to share my story at that press conference because it was part of the fight to uphold the Violence Against Women Act, to fund policies that protect people and children and help law enforcement and government assist families. I knew that telling the story again would result in more press coverage that might upset my ex-husband and kids. It was worth it this time, though. My purpose was different. During my first campaign, I told the story to deflect a political opponent. Even if he was playing dirty, I had felt dirty to address it as a candidate. But as a representative, it was my duty to advocate for others. If my story was part of that, it was my duty to share it.

The violence in my marriage is part of my life. For my children's sake, I wish it were not part of my political identity. For every American's sake, I am grateful that it is.

19.

Ground Support

Sitting on the deck crusted with salt water and sand, the bag seemed to have lost its proper place in a 1920s cigar salon. The leather satchel suitcase could have belonged to another Princeton man, F. Scott Fitzgerald, but its owner, Mike Nixon, had just set it down to hug me and be introduced to my kids. His Princeton T-shirt was hard-worn enough to leave no doubt that he was an actual graduate, and his "critter shorts" with crabs embroidered on the khaki suggested holiday weekends of gin and tonics. I made a point right then of telling Mike that he could not drink. Welcome to our wholesome family operation, I told him, putting the leather satchel in the guest room.

With about one month until the November 2018 election, I had demanded that my campaign team grant me three days of vacation with my kids. That amounted to heading to a friend's nearby beach house to minimize travel and maximize every minute of rest—or as much rest as a single mom can get with three kids and a wayward houseguest. Mike's satchel suggested a short stay, but I learned a few hours later that he had arrived on a one-way ticket to Los Angeles. We had met during the foreclosure crisis but fallen out of touch. He had turned up at a Washington, D.C., fundraiser a few weeks before, rail thin with dark crescents under his eyes. When I overheard a mutual friend tell him that he needed a change, I half-jokingly suggested that he volunteer on my campaign.

A few days later, he texted to ask for the address to give to the taxi when he arrived. I wondered how my kids would feel about having our brief local vacation interrupted by a stranger. They were weary of people picking me up for events, dropping off binders of donor calls, and prompting them to tuck in their shirts for pictures. My concerns were moot, however, as Mike did not come out of his room for nearly twenty-four hours, and only then to grab some water, sit in the sun for an hour, and go back to sleep. He was recovering and recharging, as were we. At the end of the three days, Mike threw his satchel on top of my kids' duffels and climbed into the minivan. I realized his one-way ticket was not an oversight.

After we unloaded in Irvine, I changed into a dress and headed to a campaign event. On the way out the door, I told Mike the deal: Help or head back to Washington. The campaign was running on fumes, the Republican incumbent was favored to win, and I had no time and overwhelming work to do.

• • •

My mom was a reliable Democratic voter but, like me only two years earlier, knew nothing about campaigns. She waited until only a few days before the election to arrive from Texas. This is about the worst time for a houseguest, especially one with a mother's critical eye.

"Mike!!!" I leaned over the banister, shouting to the downstairs bedroom as I pulled on a statement necklace that I hoped conveyed trustworthiness and electability. "My mom arrives today. Go get her at the airport and keep her out of my hair."

"On it!" he shouted back, as he laced up his running shoes and grabbed a bag of campaign literature. "I'm canvassing."

"And don't forget to help Paul decorate his pumpkin for the Scout contest."

"We're gonna win!" shouted Mike.

I wasn't sure if he was referring to the pumpkin contest or the campaign. Both, I hoped.

That night, about two hours later than the schedule promised, I unlocked my front door and prepared to trudge upstairs to exchange my candidate dress for pajamas. The entire house smelled of cinnamon, and I heard the clink of glasses. I looked into the living room to see Mike Nixon and my mom toasting, his arm draped over her shoulder, my mom giggling.

Paul, Betsy, and Luke are great kids with their own hobbies and interests that have nothing to do with politics. Their reactions to this book were "Oh my God, NO," "It's cringe," and "I'm gonna need to find a lawyer." They negotiated better treatment, so here is a picture of Paul behaving and looking cute. With Mike Nixon's help, this pumpkin did win.

Mike jumped up.

"Let's have pie," he said. "I made an apple pie. This wine is empty, Liz, should we open another?"

He gestured to my mom and kept talking.

"I set a new personal best at the number of doors I knocked today. The kids are asleep. Betsy left this homework for you to sign. Your mom is so great. Is Joe Biden coming tomorrow to campaign? Do you want ice cream on top? How are you?"

Mike had violated my rule about abstinence, but I could hardly begrudge him having wine while he served me his homemade pie and charmed my mom. For the last month, Mike had been a one-man rescue operation for my life. Awake and cheerful before dawn, he went for a run, supervised the kids' breakfast and departure to school, canvassed doors all day (flirting with housewives and talking taxes with Republicans), grocery shopped, cooked, and helped with homework. Thrilled to see me whenever I made it home, Mike was like a puppy with the skill set of Martha Stewart. I loved him.

My campaign staff hated him.

"Where did Katie find this guy?" I overheard them grumbling. "He's everywhere."

"Yeah," said another. "Did you see how he managed to photo-bomb Katie's picture with Joe Biden, so we had to take another? And the event was already behind schedule."

"That's not as bad as what he did with Gavin," replied someone. "He asked Gavin Newsom about his friend of a friend who knows Kimberly Guilfoyle. I mean, who is this Mike guy to say, 'Hey Governor, do you want to talk about your ex-wife or should we focus on Katie?'"

Mike had, in fact, done those things, and more. He had attended everything with endless enthusiasm, popped open the last cold drink from the campaign fridge oblivious to other thirsty staffers, led spontaneous and unwanted chants of "Katie, Katie" at rallies, and consistently grabbed a handful of swag at every campaign event.

• • •

My campaign manager, Erica, was Four-Star General Barbie. When I'd find her blond hair twisted into a knot on top of her head instead of pooling in beach waves around her shoulders, I'd know she was on her third spreadsheet of the day. Ever disciplined and organized, Erica probably was born on her due date and set an annual calendar reminder to thank her mom for delivering her. Crises were opportunities to organize a response; to-do lists were chances to check off one's accomplishments. When appendicitis surgery and antibiotics for sepsis wiped out my gut flora, Erica used my upset stomach to organize scheduled bathroom breaks to optimize my time.

Like Barbie, Erica brought a beautiful smile to an astronomical number of jobs—and did all of them well.

Erica joined the campaign when it consisted of the two of us sharing a 100-foot cubicle, and for over a year she had worked tirelessly to win. She opened four campaign offices, hired three dozen employees, and raised and spent millions of dollars. By my careful count, she made zero mistakes along the way.

Mike's shenanigans were the antithesis of Erica's discipline, but she indulged me about his constant presence. Pasting her best Sigma Kappa smile on her face, she would nod along as I analogized Mike to a winning lottery ticket. "I'm so lucky to have Mike," I would proclaim to the staff, describing how he helped me laugh off the typical kid-mom drama and folded laundry at all hours of the night. When the staff complained about Mike disrupting our routine, she would refer to what I assume came from a Mike Nixon pro-and-con list in her ubiquitous notebook.

"He canvassed again today. At least he knocks doors," she would say to placate staff. "The election is almost here. Stay focused."

Mike's boundless enthusiasm and overengagement are key traits of a campaign supervolunteer, just as Erica's discipline and control are the tools of a winning campaign manager. The naive energy of volunteers and the ruthless discipline of staffers blend together to fuel campaigns.

Professional staff treat campaigns like the term paper of their life. The outcome is victory rather than an A grade, but the tactics of all-nighters, bad coffee, and steely determination are identical. Against headwinds of apathy or outright partisan hostility, staffers only have control over the execution of their campaign tasks. They develop rigid rules and numerical metrics to soothe their nerves about facing the unpredictable, moody electorate.

For volunteers, campaigns are bewildering, thrilling experiences, akin to skydiving, that relieve the routine of their regular lives. They obsess over gear like bumper stickers, clipboards, headsets, and T-shirts. They knock on each door with excitement, wondering if they will earn a tough vote that gives them hope. Each act to help the campaign has the potential to be the difference that wins the election.

Volunteer opportunities exist because staffers cut turf, organize events, and cajole others into signing up to help. Staff can have a path to victory driven by polling, but conversations at front doors win the closest elections, and no campaign can hire enough folks to canvass without volunteers. The tension between volunteers and campaign operatives is the sticky mess of democracy. Winning takes Mike and Erica, multiplied and sustained. If you want to make a difference in a campaign, decide which one you are and get in on the action.

• • •

From spreadsheets to pies, people really do make campaigns. Mike moved in and became family, but he was simply the latest and greatest in a long string of amazing volunteers. Month after month in my campaigns, a volunteer would emerge, just as I despaired about how I'd find the energy and spirit to keep going.

In September 2017, more than a year before my first general election, a rap on our glass cubicle drew our eyes to a cheerful wave. The woman opened the door, where my sole paid staffer at the time, the long-suffering Tatiana, and I were halfway through our 150th straight day of trying to raise money.

"Hi, I'm Vicky! I'm here to volunteer. I can come whenever, as I just retired."

She plopped down in the only remaining chair and pulled on reading glasses, looking around for a task.

"I'll tell you," she continued. "Trump really pissed off the wrong people. Old hippies know how to shake shit up. How do I help?"

Asking the same question for five years and counting, Vicky still shows up. She brings me lunch when my scheduler "forgot" to find time, she's called dry cleaners on both coasts to locate a missing dress, and she has plunked my kids in her pool for the afternoon so I could work, nap, and then work some more. I could fill this whole book with a list of all the things she's done.

Vicky was joined by hundreds of others. When my mother arrived in those last few days of the campaign, she was overwhelmed at how volunteers pitched in. She kept offering war analogies.

"Look at the ground support," she'd remark. "These people are real troopers."

Just like a real army, I had every kind of volunteer, from parachuters who'd rescue me when I was a hostage at a never-ending fundraiser, to infantry who trained each day for canvassing by reviewing updated talking points. And then there were people who marched to the beat of their own drum, out of step but still in the fight.

Some volunteer ideas are pointless fun stunts, dressed up as campaigning. For example, Dawn and her friends dangled gigantic light-up letters that spelled out KATIE PORTER off a freeway overpass for months. A few cranky drivers complained that it backed up traffic, which, given the crowding on Interstate 405 in Orange County, is a specious allegation of cause and effect. Other times, volunteer help is the lifeline that you are too embarrassed to seek out. Without a supervolunteer who came over and helped me clean out my closet, I'd probably be buried alive under liberal cause T-shirts.

Sensible, thoughtful people in everyday life, volunteers can veer into inappropriate from time to time. I've had volunteers hand-deliver Spanx shapewear to my house, upset about a picture of me on social media that showed a distinct belly. Another insisted that cooking for three kids would be so easy if only I would serve tacos every Tuesday. I've received candles emblazoned with my face, leaving me uncertain what it would say about my sense of self-worth if I lit one and melted my image. I've had a group of Iranian Americans serenade me from my porch to teach me about Nowruz, leaving behind enough food to feed my kids until the next Iranian New Year.

In three campaigns, I've seen enough hijinks to script a reality television show called *Volunteers Gone Wild*. The best volunteers are willing to be helpful in any way, but that sometimes goes beyond the pale:

- Cleaning out the campaign fridge, check.

- Cleaning out my home fridge, yikes.

- Coming up with a better system to welcome people at our canvass training, check.

- Coming up to adjust my bra strap while I am speaking to an audience, yikes.

- Noting that we need name tags for folks, check.

- Noting that my middle son needs deodorant, yikes. (But not wrong!)

The boundaries between personal and political disappear in the all-consuming nature of a campaign. Sometimes I wince when my volunteers wander too far (occasionally literally) into my home, but it's a temporary, almost welcome pain, like when your mom squeezes you too tight in a hug. I could not get up in the morning to fight without knowing that I have people who volunteer— wherever and whenever I need them, and a few places and moments beyond that.

• • •

The two most polarizing words in a campaign are not "Democrat" and "Republican." The divisive duo is "lawn sign." Professional politicos recite the facts: Lawn signs do not vote; people vote. Scarce dollars and scarce time should go to canvassing and calling, connecting with humans whose fingers will hover over your and your opponent's names on Election Day.

"TV ads don't vote either," snapped one angry volunteer who was denied replacement yard signs after landscapers had tossed several from her street.

In October 2018, my staffers made T-shirts that announced ZERO LAWN SIGNS TO GIVE. In what I can only understand as part of the protest, they wore them daily without washing. Only the actual field director could authorize disbursement of the remaining weatherproof placards, stored in a locked cabinet. This was its own

These hardy heroes knocked thousands of doors and still found the energy to tussle for lawn signs.

kind of lunacy. With all the work to do in a campaign, with millions being spent on exorbitant television ads, staff are nuts to battle lawn sign fanaticism, costing ten bucks a person. But if you want to endear yourself to a campaign professional, my first tip is never to mention lawn signs.

My second recommendation is to canvass. Literally knock doors every day that ends in "y"—and twice on Sunday, as the saying goes. Volunteers often shy away from canvassing, looking for other ways to help. It cannot be the physical aspect. I've seen women snugged up in $200 worth of athleisure, fresh from boot camp followed by yoga, who refused to walk a single block to knock doors. The terror of political conversation scares volunteers toward other tasks, but democracy *is* those hard conversations. Canvassing is the greatest need of every campaign. Like online dating, it's actually fun, once you realize the worst that can happen is you hear "no." In Orange County, I can promise you a safe neighborhood, plenty of undecided voters, and a great tan from the sun. And if you knock enough doors, I'll sneak you a yard sign.

Find Your Supervolunteer Power

 Knocking doors is the best way to help a campaign. But there's more to do. These Porter Supporters' contributions might inspire you.

The Provider:
Mimi and friends put a big cooler on my porch and dropped off meals. When my kids were hungry, they'd forage for dinner.

The Coach:
Stephen, an opera singer, showed me how to project my voice without dropping into scratchy octaves. If I sounded like a 75-year-old chain-smoker by Election Day, it's because I didn't listen.

The Protector:

In my first primary, when Democrats approached to tell me to drop out, Kelly stood strong and tall, arms crossed in a protective stance.

The Energizer:

Armed with a bullhorn that somehow never ran out of batteries, Vivian led cheers that made sure everyone in a four-block radius knew I was in attendance.

The Organizer:

A customer service manager, Karen was mortified that my staffers saw voicemail as a final resting place, not a prompt for action. She answered hundreds of calls and returned messages.

The Supplier:

A new mother, Erica would add granola bars for volunteers to her cart full of diapers. Her son, "Baby Jack," has grown up along with my campaigns, from baby mascot to toddler terror to canvassing sidekick.

20.

Not Good Enough

About a week before my 2018 election, the *Pod Save America* guys came to Irvine. They planned to tape live at the University of California, Irvine, campus and timed their visit to when then former Vice President Joe Biden would be stumping. I was asked to tape a segment in a park about why canvassing and talking to voters mattered, along with Biden, who would then be filmed knocking on some doors.

I had never met Tommy Vietor and Jon Favreau. When they arrived, we shook hands and they asked some variation of the "Why run for Congress" question. I was near the end of my campaign, and I was tired.

"I just want to fix some shit," I said.

Tommy and Jon looked at each other, grinned, and high-fived me.

My response that day, replete with profanity, was definitely not my carefully rehearsed answer that I had given hundreds of times during the campaign. Especially by the end, most candidates respond by harping on why they're better than the other guy. This spares them from having to defend Congress or democracy. It makes the problem about an individual, not an institution. Substitute Tom for Jerry. Elect Ernie instead of Bert. Government, like a 1980s Timex, will keep on ticking.

But these answers obscure for voters why we have elections in the first place: as a check that our government works for us. The logic of our democracy, for all its flaws, is that government is beholden to the people. Power flows from voters to elected officials, not the inverse. The job of a candidate should be to make their case for what they'll do with that power, to stake out how Congress will serve the people. For me, that is about a government that solves problems.

• • •

One year into my time in Congress, news reports about a disease in China started to reach the United States. *The New York Times* started to graph the climbing number of infections, and we learned that "flatten the curve" was not a fitness slogan for middle-aged women at an abdominal class. Everyone seemed to have a friend of a friend whose cousin knew somebody hospitalized and on a ventilator. The news carried images of exhausted and fearful healthcare workers in makeshift protective equipment.

In those early weeks of COVID-19, the U.S. government's message was all about things not to do. *Don't travel overseas. Don't go to work. Don't send your kids to school. Don't shake hands. Don't buy supplies like hand sanitizer because there is a shortage. Don't use masks that are needed for healthcare workers. Don't go to the doctor if you are ill because it might be coronavirus and you will infect others. You might die but at least you won't spread the disease and create a pandemic.*

With all the uncertainty, Americans had no way to know if they had this new coronavirus. If you sneezed, did you have COVID-19?

If you went to the doctor, would you get a test? Would you get a big bill if it turned out you only had a cold and not COVID? The best affirmative tips from government wavered between "Do not worry" and "Wash your hands." Somehow, each one of us was supposed to find a way to use good cheer and soap to stave off a pandemic.

At the end of January, Congress scheduled its first briefing on COVID-19. Orange County had the third known COVID case in the United States, so I raced through the byzantine tunnels. I was sweating to overcome my tardiness and secure a seat in this briefing. The entrances to the auditorium were almost blocked by the number and size of ABSOLUTELY NO FOOD AND DRINK signs. Carrying an iced coffee, purchased hours before and dripping wet, I stuck it deep in my briefcase and hoped it did not spill. I took a deep breath and threw open the door.

Every eye in the room was on me. When there are only a dozen people in a huge auditorium, even one person can make a grand entrance. Far from having to stand in the back, I had about one-quarter of the auditorium to myself. I was reassured that whatever exactly "social distancing" was, I was likely doing it successfully in that moment.

The nation's top public health experts and relevant administration officials were proffering careful talking points, ranging from basic science by doctors ("This disease is caused by germs") to complete nonsense by Trump appointees. The State Department people refused to answer questions, only offering repeated statements that they were "monitoring the situation." Given that this sounded awfully similar to scrolling through one's email instead of working, I was not reassured.

Devices are banned in classified briefings, so I dug a pen out of the bottom of my bag and scribbled notes on the back of my speech from an earlier event. When I left, I grabbed my phone and texted my sister, Dr. Emily Porter.

"We are all going to die," I wrote.

"Too bad Trump's f***ing wall cannot protect against coronavirus," she replied.

"At least the guy who heads up Infectious Diseases at NIH seemed good. I trust him," I said.

Then I sent her a Wikipedia link to Anthony S. Fauci.

• • •

Congress's arrival on the scene of a problem makes me look like the OG Early Bird. Even as full shutdowns took effect in California and some states, Congress operated as usual. The only sign of a looming pandemic was the continuation of biweekly update briefings. The same dozen members showed up, making the auditorium feel like an early morning class with an unpopular professor. Most of my colleagues failed to see the scope of harm the virus could create, not connecting its risks to their legislative duties.

It took three months of death and suffering for Congress to finally have a hearing on COVID-19. On March 12, 2020, at 10:00 A.M., in the walnut-paneled Oversight Committee room, top federal officials raised their right hands and swore to tell the truth, the whole truth, and nothing but the truth.

One after the other, my colleagues asked what could be done to stop the spread of this coronavirus. Looking through their wire-rim glasses to consult notes, the experts acknowledged the problems that my colleagues described. I waited, impatient for my turn.

Seniority in Congress determines not just which office you occupy and which committees you serve on, but also the order of members' questions at hearings. This means that sometimes the most junior members, like me, get silenced entirely. Time runs out, and witnesses leave before we come up in the queue.

At this first COVID-19 hearing, I was the newest addition to the

Oversight and Reform Committee. I joined a year after starting Congress when members died and resigned, creating openings. That day, I was second-to-last in line. Forty-three congressmembers were ahead of me in seniority to ask questions.

The previous week, I had sent a letter to Dr. Robert Redfield, the head of the Centers for Disease Control and Prevention (CDC). My healthcare staffer, Jessica Seigel, a neurotic genius and true dork, had found a provision in the Code of Federal Regulations that allowed the CDC to order free testing for any disease in a public health emergency, regardless of insurance status. After Dr. Redfield blew past the deadline to respond, I was ready to follow up with him at the hearing.

A few minutes before noon, the gavel suddenly banged, sending the hearing into recess. The Trump administration had called the witnesses to a meeting at the White House. The hearing was cut short at only two hours—and we had barely gotten halfway down the dais in seniority. It wasn't clear when or if they'd be back. The senior members of the committee had asked their questions, and the witnesses could legitimately say that they had shown up.

That day, I had bigger problems than not getting a straight answer from a witness. I didn't even get to ask a question.

Without a way to restart the hearing, I resolved to send a follow-up letter to Dr. Redfield. The odds seemed slim that he would respond, given that he had ignored my prior letter and had just appeared before the committee.

With the Oversight hearing having abruptly ended, I went over to my other committee, Financial Services, for its hearing. Votes were called, I did a media interview, and I took a few meetings. In mid-March, Congress was doing what the nation was: pretending that coronavirus would not upend our lives. But friends kept texting me pictures of empty grocery shelves, and I knew that if I did not get home to hoard Cinnamon Toast Crunch, my kids would make my life more miserable than Washington, D.C., ever could.

That afternoon, Chairwoman Carolyn Maloney announced that the witnesses would return the next day to continue the hearing. I never confirmed how that happened, but I guarantee you that it was the work of a dogged Oversight staffer, who will never get enough credit for doing their job.

My staffer Jessica was a lot like the Oversight staffer and did not let go of urgent questions that needed answers. She suggested an unusual course of action, and I took it. I tipped my hand. The night between the first and second parts of the hearing, we emailed the CDC staff to remind them of our letter. We advised them that I would question the CDC director about the regulation that permitted the government to give free testing in public health situations.

• • •

"The gentlelady from California, Ms. Porter, is recognized for five minutes."

I sat in my place in the farthest corner of the dais, in the bottom row, against the far wall. I reached down and hauled out a whiteboard, narrowly missing Deb Haaland, the only member of the Oversight Committee with even less seniority than me. I scribbled numbers unevenly on the whiteboard, angling my handwriting up and down, despite my efforts at neatness. I asked about the costs of diagnosing COVID: How much to get a CBC panel? How much for a Flu A test? How much for an ER visit for high-severity illness?

Dr. Robert Kadlec, the Assistant Secretary for Preparedness and Response at the Department of Health and Human Services, was wildly off on the estimated costs. Like a losing *Price Is Right* contestant, he underestimated and then lost the show by going way over in some answers. I kept at it, summing up the costs to illustrate $1,331 as a conservative price tag for COVID testing in an emergency room. That was a number that most Americans, insured or uninsured, could not afford.

Halfway through my allotted five minutes for questioning, I turned to CDC director Robert Redfield, the nation's top doctor. Seated between a not-yet-famous Dr. Fauci and Dr. Kadlec, Director Redfield had an advantage that students in my classes never got. I had told him the question in advance. With less than three minutes on the clock, I asked him to make COVID testing free.

"We're going to do everything to make sure that everybody can get the care they need," he said.

His answer of "doing everything," in translation from Washington-speak to real people's lives, was certainly not doing enough. I had three kids, three thousand miles away and scared. I was scared. The cost of COVID testing was high enough that I knew I would second-guess whether to test my own kids or myself if we had a runny nose or a cough.

"Nope, not good enough," I interrupted. "Reclaiming my time. Dr. Redfield, you have the existing authority. Will you commit right now to using the authority that you have, vested in you, under law, that provides in a public health emergency for testing, treatment, exam, isolation, without cost? Yes or no?"

"What I can say is that I'm going to review it in detail," he replied, a bit testy that I had cut him off.

I lifted up my copy of the regulation, hoping that nobody would notice my hands trembling. I had one minute left.

I pressed again: "The deadline and the time for delay has passed. Will you commit to invoking your existing authority under 42 C.F.R. 71.30 to provide for coronavirus testing for every American regardless of insurance coverage?"

Dr. Redfield responded, "What I was trying to say is that CDC is working with HHS now to see how we operationalize that."

I dropped my voice and slowed for Dr. Redfield to hear every word. "I hope that that answer weighs heavily on you, because it is going to weigh very heavily on me and on every American family."

With my time about to expire, I turned away from the witnesses and began to collect my papers.

But Dr. Redfield was not content to let me drop the mic with my guilt trip. He wanted to recover, to reestablish himself as Government-in-Charge.

"Our intent is to make sure that every American gets the care and treatment they need at this time during this major epidemic," he said placatingly. "We are currently working with HHS to see how to best operationalize it."

I hate words like "operationalize"—and Dr. Redfield had used that God-awful word not once, but twice. Even more, I hate what operationalize means. For years during the foreclosure crisis, I had watched families lose their homes while big banks "operationalized" mortgage assistance programs. As a consumer protection lawyer, I had listened to corporate executives explain away their outright scams in depositions as mere errors in "operationalizing" the law. As I had confessed that campaign morning to the *Pod Save America* guys, I want government to get shit done, not ponder how to do that. No alphabet soup of interagency procedures was going to reassure a sick American that they could get—and afford to get—a test.

As is so stereotypically true in Washington, a government bureaucrat was offering big words and false bravado, instead of an actual answer and a real solution. The little light in front of me had turned from green to yellow, as only seconds remained in my five-minute question period. It was over. I had failed to "operationalize" getting a straight answer.

In Congress, instead of brusquely interrupting you, the Chair uses a gavel. She taps quietly once or twice, and then if needed, loudly. I waited for that sound, sentencing me to live with "operationalize" as the best that government could offer.

In that little slice of silence, I decided to press on. As I had told Dr. Redfield, his answer was not good enough. The law was enacted for this exact situation; the CDC just needed to use it.

"Dr. Redfield, you don't need to do any work to operationalize. You need to make a commitment to the American people, so they come in to get tested." I looked him in the eye. "You can operationalize the payment structure tomorrow."

Dr. Redfield whispered with his aide, and then responded, "I think you're an excellent questioner, so the answer is yes."

That last single word gave Americans a tool against COVID: the ability to get a free test.

• • •

In those early months of the pandemic, as Americans were dying and the disease was winning, the message of the Trump administration was that widespread testing simply wasn't feasible. Our only tool to stop it was to literally hide in our homes. At every plea for help, in answer to every question about what could be done, our government had said "no."

Even in the first hours of the congressional hearing, the experts had deflected, folding their hands like a steeple in front of themselves and incanting that there was nothing more that could be done. Dr. Redfield and the other bureaucrats had intoned thousands of learned words in those two days of hearings. His "yes" was literally the only word that mattered to Americans. In fighting and winning that answer from him, I got our government to do its job.

In the next moment after his acquiescence, I did something I'd never done before in a congressional hearing. Sitting in the last row of the hearing room, I turned to the television cameras and spoke straight to the American people: "Everybody in America hear that? You are eligible to go get tested. Do not let cost be a barrier."

When the CDC director made that commitment to me, I wanted the American people to know that the promise was to them. That "yes" would not make a difference if it reverberated in the hearing room but Americans did not hear it.

When I questioned the CDC director, only 3,498 Americans had been tested for COVID-19. Just over two weeks later, by March 27, 2020, over 100,000 Americans were tested in a single week. In the months ahead, that number continued to grow.

• • •

In America, we each get what we deserve, so the theory goes. Pull yourself up by your bootstraps. If you get fired, get sick, or lose your job: That is your problem. You, an individual, need to do better.

During the early months of the pandemic, it was the same message. Each of us was charged with preventing the spread of this new disease. The problem was an individual one; we each just needed to not get sick. Our collective power, held by the government, was being directed at reminding us that our fates were in our own hands (and whether we washed them).

But individuals don't have the ability to deliver public health tools. Government exists exactly for far-reaching dangers like a war or a pandemic. We elect leaders and give government resources so that it can solve problems that we cannot solve ourselves, no matter how much good ol' fashioned American willpower we each apply.

When a government leader says that they are working to operationalize next steps, that is a slow road to nowhere. That answer shows a lack of belief in government and a lack of will from that leader to make government work.

Decades before, Congress had passed a law to address public health emergencies. It allowed the government to pick up the tab for testing precisely because we need to act together. We cannot beat back a pandemic by ourselves, any more than we can win a war with only one soldier. By combining resources and coordinating action, government fixes shit that we individually never could. That is why I want to serve in Congress. And if I ever stop having that answer to the question, tell me, "Not good enough." And vote me out.

21.

An Orange County Family

My first day in Congress was my forty-fifth birthday, and I was representing the 45th District of California. It all seemed to fit, I thought, as I boarded the gilded MEMBERS ONLY elevator in the Capitol. On January 3, 2019, I was making my first trip to the House floor for the members' swearing-in ceremony.

I did not recognize the two other members in the elevator. They wore dark suits and red ties. Republicans, I guessed? One gentleman asked where I was from.

"Iowa," I replied, with a nervous smile.

"Hmm," he said, looking puzzled. "Who did you beat to get here?"

As the words "Mimi Walters" came out of my mouth, I realized my mistake in identifying myself. Mimi Walters had represented Orange County, California.

The elevator chimed, and we pressed into the crowded hall approaching the House floor. I was saved by the bell from having to explain that I was originally "from" Iowa, but currently from California's 45th District.

My inclination to answer "Iowa" reflected my Midwestern roots.

In rural America, "Where are you from?" means *Where are your people from?* and not *Where do you live?* In such small towns, you know where everyone lives, and nobody ever visits on vacation. Union County, Iowa, isn't exactly Disneyland at spring break. As a fifth-generation Iowan, I am certainly "from Iowa" in the origin story sense.

My answer also revealed that I was nervous. Congress is an intimidating place, and it had been so uncertain whether I'd win that I had never envisioned myself physically in the U.S. Capitol—let alone what I would say once I got there.

Justifications aside, that was the politically stupidest answer to a question that I had given in two years of hard campaigning. People in California's 45th District had just entrusted me to fight for their interests in Washington, D.C., and I couldn't even identify myself as the congressmember from Orange County. If I repeated my slipup from the elevator in public, my political career would end abruptly.

"California," I chastised myself. "You are a Californian. You are *from* California." Looking around the House of Representatives that first day, I marveled that I had gotten there. I often felt the same way in California. Driving my minivan past blooming birds-of-paradise and the turquoise ocean while running mundane errands, I would wonder how I was in heaven but alive and well. Maybe I didn't immediately offer up that I was from California because it seems unlikely that such a blindingly beautiful place would send forth an everyday chubby brunette like me. But California had welcomed my family and me ten years prior. *I am a Californian,* I think in disbelief every morning when I feel the sunshine on my face.

• • •

In 2009, when I was recruited to the University of California, Irvine, I had no idea where Orange County was. The entirety of my

Southern California experience was a disorienting layover at the international terminal at LAX (where, I swear, I saw somebody attempt to check a live chicken as baggage).

But the university recruiters were prepared to sell Irvine, and I was ready to buy. I was living elsewhere in California, teaching at the law school at the University of California, Berkeley. The damp gray there was sinking my spirits, and judgy parents would frown at me for letting my kids eat Cheetos and run wild while I read *The Wall Street Journal* on a bench in the playground.

With strip malls at every intersection, Irvine had none of the funky, earthy pretensions of the East Bay. The University of California, Irvine, and its home city were growing rapidly, but careful planning was anticipating and accommodating the community's needs. It's said that to keep everyone happy, a university president must deliver sex for students, sports for alumni, and parking for faculty. While UC Irvine was perhaps struggling in the first two categories, hours waiting in the Berkeley drizzle for a public bus made me ogle its southern cousin's convenient parking lot. The law school dean

Beach and baby, Corona del Mar, 2011.

laughed when I asked about the length of the waiting list for faculty parking; I can include a pass in your offer letter, he replied.

I accepted the job, and we moved in July 2011 to Irvine. My daughter, Betsy, was born a few months later, becoming the first native Californian in my extended family. I felt that fate had brought me to the University of Iowa in time to make my sons sixth-generation Iowans, but Betsy's birthright to the beach marked a new direction for our lives. We celebrated Christmas Day in 2011 at Big Corona Beach, setting up our new sunshade for Betsy to nap under while the boys dug in the sand.

• • •

If my elevator slipup on day one of Congress had not focused my mind on being from California, the nineteen-hour round-trip commute from Washington, D.C., to Orange County was serving that purpose. California might as well be another country, I cursed, noting that I could have commuted from London more quickly and with less jet lag. The country should run itself around its population center, California, I fumed. This was a distinctly non-Iowan worldview. As I'd wake up at 4:00 A.M. to start my days on Washington's schedule, I disparaged East Coast elites for running Congress on Eastern time, ignoring my own happy years in Massachusetts, New York, and Connecticut.

I made twenty one-way trips between D.C. and California in my first fifteen weeks serving in Congress before I told myself there must be a better way. *Box up a few things,* I told my kids, *this fall we are going to try living in Virginia. It'll be great,* I promised. *You'll love seeing the leaves change colors, visiting the historic sites, and learning about a new part of the country.*

The trouble started before I had even finished paying the taxi driver who took us from Reagan National Airport to our rental row house in Old Town, Alexandria. Betsy was splayed out flat on the sidewalk, sobbing. "What happened?" I cried, as if it were a mystery that she had fallen.

"These sidewalks are shit, Mom," said fourteen-year-old Luke, pointing to the undulating layer of bricks that made up the Alexandria sidewalk, which had been pushed up and caved down by tree roots and the freeze-thaw cycle over decades.

"It's not 'shit.' It's historic," I snapped at Luke, while I dusted Betsy off. We hauled our witness-relocation-sized suitcases up the front steps and tried life as California transplants.

In the next months, as my kids opined on Virginia's shortcomings compared to our neighborhood in Irvine, I realized the other drawback of becoming Californians. My kids were soft. The heaven of Southern California had primed them to equate the purgatory of our trial period in Virginia with confinement to hell.

When we hit a sizable pothole driving to school, Paul wondered, "Why do they use potholes when they could have speed bumps?" The idea of poor road maintenance was wholly unfamiliar to him, and he believed potholes were intentional traffic calming, akin to the landscaped contoured medians in Irvine.

My kids' exploration of the neighborhood didn't turn up a single community pool, despite the humidity of that September, and they were robbed of a legitimate holiday when they had to go to school on Cesar Chavez Day. At school, kids accused Paul of lying when he said he had never visited Universal Studios and called Luke a "gay Cali hippie" when he called out incessant homophobic slurs.

Luke rallied his siblings to demand that we move back to California before Chinese New Year, so they didn't miss out on red envelopes of celebratory cash. He asserted that his school was racist because there were no Asian students in his class when "half of America is Asian," reflecting the demographics of Irvine, not the United States.

The kids were shocked to discover that on Halloween, they needed coats on top of their costumes for trick-or-treating.

"You don't wear a coat because it messes up your costume," Betsy told me. "That's why Halloween is in October when it's warm in California." I gently explained to her that in most of the United States, Halloween marked the arrival of cold weather.

"That's weird," she responded, heading out bare-legged into the forty-degree night in her paper-thin Harley Quinn costume.

Earlier in the day, I'd had my own encounter with different coastal traditions for Halloween. In California, many people dress in costume all day; heck, in West Hollywood, many people are

Rep. Alexandria Ocasio-Cortez snapped this shot of Batgirl. The only person in costume, I was undeterred, as this smile shows.

barely clad every day. I donned my Batgirl costume that morning, making sure my cape met the dress code by covering my shoulders. When I arrived at the Financial Services Committee meeting, I discovered in real time that the House of Representatives is not a workplace that celebrates the holiday. As the sole person showing Halloween spirit, I brought a superhero level of cheer to the dreary legislative markup.

The final straw came when a nor'easter flooded the basement that served as Luke's bedroom. Mopping up the rainwater and discovering black mold behind the built-in shelves, I had to agree with the kids—this mess would never happen in Southern California. Having moved about every two years between high school and my mid-forties, I expected myself to cheerfully adapt to Virginia and set an example for my family. But Virginia felt unfamiliar, and that made life there hard in its own way. I had traded an easy commute to work for an uneasy sense of dislocation.

It turned out that my kids shared the perspectives of my constituents, who believed that terrific public schools, diversity, and amazing outdoor recreation were the good life and California was where to find it. My life in Irvine was a testament to the California promise of a better life that has drawn generations to the West. Job security came with the tenured professorship; a healthier, happier family began when Orange County adjudicated my divorce; and balancing work and family was possible because the community offered terrific childcare and a two-minute commute to work. In my years in Orange County, I had relaxed into my identities as mother, professor, and policymaker.

My dad, an Iowa lifer, once astutely observed that being a meteorologist for Orange County, deciding whether to predict 68 degrees or 72 degrees every day of the year, must be the most numbingly uneventful job. But I missed uneventful; or, more precisely, I missed being in the place that had been the backdrop for my surviving so many life events. On my monthly trips back to Orange County to work in the district, I would point out family landmarks to my accompanying staffer: the park where I celebrated my first Mother's Day as a single parent, the church where I received my award for Cub Scout Leader of the Year, the Macy's where I lost Luke and found him hiding safely in a clothing rack, and the bakery that lovingly made each of Betsy's seven birthday cakes to date.

In December, only a few months after we'd left, we returned to California. The kids were welcomed back to their Irvine public school, rejoined their Scout activities, and returned to bickering about whether we should go to the pool or the beach on Sunday afternoons. Nothing about Irvine had changed, but neither had anything about Congress's terrorizing schedule or the commute that came with it. When I explained that I needed more help if I was going to manage the long flights and jet lag, the kids promised to take on household chores—and do them regularly without complaint. We negotiated allowances, and Paul announced that he would gladly be my "laundry boy" if it meant we could stay in California.

As my second year in Congress began in 2020, I was on the ballot for reelection to keep "fighting for Orange County families." That mantra felt accurate to me, despite being sort of cheesy. Living in Virginia, we learned that we were an Orange County family. My campaign slogan was both an acknowledgment of my past accomplishments and a promise for my future work. I hoped that I would find a way to be a Californian, a congressmember, and a mom, instead of having to choose among them. But I was steadfast that I would rather leave Congress to stay in California than leave California to stay in Congress.

Even if I spent more time on an airplane and in the U.S. Capitol than I did in the pristine strip malls and playgrounds of Irvine, California was home. Trying to relocate across the country was letting my new job in Congress supplant who I was as a mother and a person. California was the place where I fit together the pieces of my adult life, and I felt secure there, snugged in by my experiences and community.

· · ·

That sense of security would be tested a few months later by COVID-19.

On March 11, 2020, President Trump halted international travel from Europe, and I worried that the same would happen to domestic travel before I could get home to California. Congress slowed its work, adding days to my stay in Washington. The urgency of addressing the looming pandemic increased, but each day crawled by as the legislation grew bloated with additional programs.

At the same time, back in California, grocery shelves were emptying, and most businesses were shutting their doors. My friends were texting me that they had found toilet paper or frozen kid-friendly food at a particular Target, but rather than adding to our stash, my kids were depleting our supplies. Irvine schools announced they would cease classes beginning on Monday.

On Saturday, March 14, 2020, I voted until after midnight, napped a few hours, and flew home. My kids were scared to hug me because they were afraid that I had caught COVID (they were prescient to believe the U.S. Capitol was a super-spreader location). The next morning, I started our pandemic preparations. I downloaded a reading app and books for all of us from the public library and joined a grocery group of families to limit our shopping trips. I repurposed my whiteboard for a daily COVID kids' briefing, with reminders to put used cloth masks into the hamper.

California was my family's place of protection during the pandemic. Although we were away from its beaches, off its well-maintained roads, and without its childcare programs, we appreciated our home in different ways. Our schools handed out devices for remote learning, our grocery stores stayed open even when short-staffed, and our state and county leaders prioritized testing and prevention. The pandemic raised the stakes of having elected leaders who understood what communities needed—in real time and for real families. Living in California through the pandemic made me its representative in a stronger, sharper way, as I saw how our family and community struggled and survived.

I have not doubted since that day in March, when I was desperate to get to my family and to Irvine, that I am from Orange County, California. Every trip to Washington is a visit; every trip back is a homecoming. Californians will decide whether I am in Congress for a year or a decade, but I will forever be in California.

22

The Work

People always want to know if I like being in Congress.

"The job sucks," I tell them, watching their eyes go wide at my matter-of-fact statement. Politicians are supposed to talk about how being elected is the greatest honor of their life or some other cliché.

"But the work is amazing," I admit.

Unless some staffer is tugging me away, I take a few minutes to explain why these two assessments aren't contradictory.

When you think about taking a new job, you assess the opportunities for promotion, the salary, the benefits, your co-workers, your commute, and your daily duties. Congress is lousy on these metrics. Allow me to illustrate:

- **Opportunities for advancement:** Most people work in hope of a promotion, but dying was the next rung on the ladder for 9 percent of departing congresspeople during my second term. Sure, a couple became cabinet secretaries or senators, but odds are you lose your election or you die—or worse, you lose your soul and become a lobbyist.

- **Co-workers:** Would you go to work every day if you knew
  you had to share office space with Marjorie Taylor Greene?
  Or would you polish up your résumé to avoid her Jewish
  Space Lasers or other crazy shit? Right, I thought so.

- **Commute:** Unlike Joe Biden, who let Amtrak rock him to
  sleep each night on the way home, many congressmembers
  spend twenty hours a week commuting by plane. Even by the
  worst suburban sprawl metrics, this is a super-commute.
  Spending nearly half of a normal forty-hour workweek in a
  metal can in the sky—where the excitement is "pretzel or
  cookie?"—just blows.

Despite the job falling short by most measures, the work of Congress is the best experience of my professional life. When I say "work of Congress," it's important to define that. I emphatically do not mean voting, which is the least rewarding work in Congress. Voting involves racing to the House floor against the ticking time to stand in line to hit a little green YES button or a red NO button. Endure the scrum of the mingling and glad-handing on the House floor, repeat a few times, and you've lost two hours of your life. Ninety-nine percent of the time, everybody already knows how everybody will vote and what the outcome will be. Voting is so easy a child can do it. When my son Luke was twelve years old, he accompanied me to the House floor for an entire week. He obtained the list of bills for consideration, studied it carefully, and watched the process. He offered up two observations:

"They don't want you to think about your vote. It says **'VOTE YES'** in huge letters. How could you screw that up?"

And, he continued, "I guess they have to tell you what to do since nobody but me is reading what we're voting on."

True statements, my fine son.

As I see it, the real work of Congress is civic education. Democracy only functions if voters know what's going on in their government and elected representatives know what's going on in their communities. As a congressmember, that means teaching and learning, respectively.

The American people set the nation's agenda every two years with House elections, and every four years with presidential elections. They cannot decide if they support a government policy without first knowing what the government is doing (or not doing). Representatives should be teachers, with constituents as our students.

At the same time, we should also be students, learning from our constituents. Without knowing the challenges and ideas of the people we represent, congressmembers can only substitute their own views for voters' views. While that may happen, it is not how representative democracy is supposed to work. Getting the facts, doing the research, and gaining experience are moments of learning that help me make the best votes for my community.

Teaching and learning are the exact work I did as a law professor, before I ran for Congress. I loved that, and so not surprisingly, I love Congress work.

$$\bullet \;\; \bullet \;\; \bullet$$

As a professor, I always entered the classroom with a lesson plan. I approach the teaching part of my Congress job the exact same way. To help people learn, I explain things and use vocabulary that is appropriate for everyone, regardless of background. To engage them, I strategize how to be entertaining and informational. I'll use impeachment to illustrate this work.

When Special Counsel Robert Mueller released his report on Russian interference in the 2016 election, most Democrats reviewed the report and came to the same conclusion: Ample material evidence suggested that President Trump obstructed justice on eleven occasions, and such abuses of power were grounds for impeachment.

Armed with this knowledge, most Democrats sprang into action: refreshing Twitter to check @Politics_Polls for updates on the partisan winds, or fundraising off President Trump's wrongdoing. Even worse, prominent Democrats exhorted the public to "read the Mueller Report" and lamented voters' supposed failure to understand the issues at hand.

Folks, that kind of demand on workers, parents, students, retirees, and other voters is outrageous. A representative's job is to learn the facts and issues, take a position, and then educate the public. Rather than decrying the lack of civic engagement, I did the work. I studied the Mueller Report with a staffer to digest its findings and reviewed scholarship on impeachment from legal experts. Once my mind was made up, I readied myself to teach.

Lesson Plan for Impeachment, May 2019

- **Objectives for constituents:**

  - Understand impeachment process, especially the role of House

  - Know facts that establish the president's acts of obstruction of justice

  - Identify next steps for Congress in obtaining information

- **Strategy:** direct-to-camera video, kept short and delivered slowly, distributed by social media channels

- **Key vocabulary:** impeachment, obstruction of justice, subpoena power, high crimes and misdemeanors

- **Materials needed:** video equipment, teleprompter

- **Additional resources:** Frequently Asked Questions document to address issues not covered in the video, talking points for staff answering phones, constituent correspondence that links to video and FAQ

- **Assessment:** Engagement with video including views, comments, and shares; number and type of constituent comments; feedback at town halls

The script should've been the most difficult part. Contrary to what some wingnuts think, merely carrying a copy of the Constitution in your coat pocket or waving it around at press conferences does not make you an expert. The Constitution is hard; people devote their professional lives to studying it. My job was to help people learn the vocabulary and process, to provide a point of entry for their thinking and a foundation for their opinions.

The best advice I got when I started teaching law was that students are not detectives, and the classroom is not the scene of a mystery. I didn't hide the lesson in Congress either, because my constituents are not mind readers. In the first few seconds of the video, I simply said, "I have decided to support an impeachment investigation."

While that sentence was simple, getting it on tape was hard. While other Democrats in tough races contorted themselves to maneuver the perceived political consequences of impeachment, my struggles were mundane but intractable: complete, repeated technology fails.

Interpretations of the Constitution are not shoot-from-the-hip conversations. To accurately deliver our carefully written script, I wanted to use a teleprompter. Reading from the screen let me focus on tone and pacing, rather than searching my memory for the next phrase. The first effort was in my living room with an easily flustered staffer, trying to deploy a newly purchased teleprompter designed for use with a cell phone. We failed because I could not read the tiny letters on the phone screen. When we blew up the font, the phone could only show one word at a time. I wanted to emphasize my wording, but Not. Like. This. Which is how it sounded as I waited for each word to appear on the little screen.

We tried again when I traveled to D.C., with a teleprompter that used an iPad. The text was readable, and I looked gravely into the camera and delivered the script perfectly. Nobody will ever fully appreciate my performance because nobody will ever hear it. The microphone was plugged in the wrong hole. No sound.

The third try indeed proved the charm. My staff and I went pleading to the House Democratic Caucus to use their studio and equipment, and we created a video that explained the evidence for impeachment and the next steps in an inquiry.

Our tech troubles created a month of delay. The video was released on June 17, 2019. Even with that, I was the first Democrat with a tough reelection race—thus designated a "Frontline" member—to publicly support impeachment. Many members warned me of the folly of taking a stand. On the day I announced my decision, one Democrat told me, "Enjoy your one term."

Buddy, I sure did. I enjoyed my first term in Congress because I stood up for democracy and had confidence in my constituents to do the same.

Members like Stephen Lynch, in a safe Democratic seat for two decades, even accused those who supported impeachment of somehow being Trump allies.

"You are going to give Donald Trump another four years by doing that. You are helping him. . . . That's what I know in my heart," he lectured in August 2019.

Accusing fellow Americans of political mischief is a far cry from trusting them to stand up for our country.

Speaker Nancy Pelosi and other tough-seat Frontliners argued that the American people needed to support impeachment first, before we as their representatives could do so. They thought the American people lacked consensus and we should wait for it to emerge. I differed on the strategy. Lamenting a lack of support is quite different than trying to build it. By teaching people the facts and the law, I invited them to reach their own conclusions about impeachment. Many would agree, and many would not. Respect between those two camps is built on a shared understanding of the facts of the Mueller Report, the history of the Constitution, and the steps in the impeachment process.

Impeachment did not begin until months later, on September 24, 2019, following a whistleblower coming forward. Evidence showed that President Trump tried to withhold security assistance to Ukraine in return for political favors. While impeachment ultimately failed in the Senate, my vote created little political risk for me. My constituents knew where I stood—and why—as I had spent months educating them about impeachment and learning their concerns at town halls, in constituent correspondence, and on the phones.

Although divisive, impeachment was an easy topic to teach because the public were excited students about this rare event. Not all topics in Congress are as sexy as impeachment. Then again, my favorite course to teach as a law professor was something called the Uniform Commercial Code. (I had a catchphrase for most key topics. For example, when repossessing a car: "The nighttime is the right time.") My prior teaching was eighth-grade math, where I taught coordinate graphing with Battleship games. Not all important subjects, like Medicare enrollment or regressive tax policy, are entertaining or familiar. As a teacher, sometimes you have to bring the party.

• • •

"Keep calling," I barked. "There has to be one."

I had an upcoming virtual town hall to teach my constituents about President Biden's proposed budget. With roughly $1.5 trillion to map out, I needed a large whiteboard. In my district office in Orange County, I painted an entire wall with whiteboard paint. The Office of the Architect of the Capitol was resistant to my big whiteboard energy, however, so when in Washington, I only had small sizes.

"Did you try Ways and Means? The tax folks surely like numbers."

No dice.

"What about the Democratic Caucus? Put out an SOS to the entire Dem Schedulers LISTSERV."

No response.

Fact: The U.S. House of Representatives does not own a single large whiteboard. As someone who uncaps an Expo marker with the zeal of a medieval Crusader drawing his sword, I felt set up for defeat. My work as a representative was to teach the bills and policies, and teachers need classroom supplies.

As a professor, I frequently encountered a tragedy of the commons with the whiteboard. Instead of throwing out dried-up markers, colleagues would just leave them on the whiteboard tray. I would toss them in the trash, and my students purchased me sets of new markers as end-of-semester gifts, so I could bring my own. Thoughtless colleagues failed to erase the board, leaving me fuming about lost teaching time as I wiped it clean. Every classroom, though, did have a whiteboard.

Despite allocating itself $1.4 billion each year, Congress lacks this tool of the trade of a teacher—a huge whiteboard. That sad fact reveals the underlying truth: My colleagues do not think their work is to educate constituents. Their thinking (I won't call it logic) seems to be that as representatives, it's enough if they themselves understand. They'll do the thinking for the rest of us.

"This is bullshit!" I shouted when my staff advised that their herculean efforts had not turned up an appropriately sized whiteboard.

Ingenious and industrious, they grouped four small whiteboards together as a makeshift substitute. During my town hall, I drew simple lists of increased budget items and decreased budget items compared to prior years. I noted key dollar figures and circled things for emphasis. With teaching tools like a whiteboard, I highlighted key points and boosted engagement. Lessons do not have to be learned the hard way.

Congress has a big responsibility to educate the public as part of a functioning democracy. It needs a big-ass whiteboard to match. Our office has purchased a whiteboard for Congress to have going forward. It's on wheels, so ask your representative to borrow it and get to work.

· · ·

I missed the first days of official orientation to Congress because my race was undecided as ballots were counted to determine a winner. When I finally arrived, I boarded the morning bus for the U.S. Capitol from the Holiday Inn, ready to learn. It took only about ten seconds for me to get the boot.

The staffer for the "Republican bus" advised me that I might be more comfortable on the "Democratic bus," which boarded around the corner. I dutifully climbed down and boarded the Democratic bus—which was the exact same, right down to the plush upholstery, an ecumenical red and blue stripe. I didn't notice any extra padding as I settled into the seat. Clearly, the staffer had been referencing the mood, not the physical bus condition, in terms of my comfort.

The partisan divide in transportation continued during the orientation. We came together only briefly for sessions on security and protocol, which were so filled with acronyms and jargon that I could hardly follow. Most of our time was spent attending separate caucus meetings, in which senior folks jockeyed for leadership. It was not educational at all, except in teaching me that politicking did not end after the election.

Given the lack of substance in the orientation, I feared that I would have to learn the hard way, through on-the-job mistakes as a representative. I had declined an unofficial orientation hosted at Harvard because it was sponsored by large corporations. I already had a pretty good idea what those companies wanted: fewer regulations on every industry that wanted to cheat, pollute, or rip off taxpayers.

The Library of Congress, founded to educate Congress, came to the rescue. Its three-day orientation was bipartisan and substantive. We learned the magic of budget reconciliation to escape the oppression of the Senate filibuster and fund the government. Librarians led sessions on immigration law, Social Security, environmental law, and other topics. At a session on the defense budget, I caused gasps from military-minded colleagues when I raised my hand to ask how the Pentagon could ensure price competition when half of its spending goes to just two companies, Lockheed and Boeing. Such basic facts were inviting questions that I thought needed to be asked, and I set out to look for anyone other than lobbyists to teach me.

After those three days, learning was mostly haphazard. My colleague Jamie Raskin had an amazing program on how to question in hearings, and was incredulous when I was one of only a half dozen members to show up. *You could give this* presentation, he observed, and asked what I was thinking: *Where the hell is everyone else?*

The work of Congress may be teaching, but to do that, one has to learn the material first. As a law professor, I split my time between research and teaching, and I took the same approach in Congress. Committee staff prepared ten-page briefings for each hearing topic, which my staff supplemented with research reports and data. As a child, I got free books from the nonprofit Reading Is Fundamental. I took the message to heart, devouring every page. Many nights, I fell asleep with a binder on my face while preparing for the next day's work.

I followed the Offices of the Inspectors General on Twitter, clicking on any report that seemed to present oversight opportunities. I barraged my legislative staff with newspaper articles. I read a special report in the *Los Angeles Times* about Cold War nuclear testing in the Marshall Islands, learning that the United States detonated bombs there with a yield equivalent to roughly 1.6 Hiroshima-sized bombs every day for twelve years. In 2021, the dozen government agencies in charge of coordinating an ongoing strategic relationship with the Marshall Islands were trying to wash their hands of our nuclear legacy and pointing fingers at each other. I sent letters, had meetings, did press, conducted oversight hearings, and pushed successfully for the appointment of a special envoy to reset the negotiation. Aggrieved officials at the State Department and Department of Energy speculated on how I'd gotten engaged on this issue. They asked which lobbyist had approached me—and were surprised when I pointed to the news article. Reading is fundamental to a congressmember's work.

• • •

Sometimes representatives read about problems, but usually they see them or hear them. The press scrum that harasses representatives for spicy quotes opines that "Congress goes on vacation" when we head to our districts. Actually, the D.C. press corps is who gets time off when the legislative session adjourns; we do our most valuable learning in our communities.

On district workweeks, I've met with student veterans about how to support their education, visited the Chipotle test kitchen to discuss automation and food safety, tested a game-like invention to help stroke patients rehabilitate better, and walked onto an overpass under construction to see the danger that carpenters face as cars speed past.

Washington insiders, including lobbyists and House leadership, would prefer that congressmembers *not know* things, because that might distract us from their priorities—too often bought and paid for by big corporations. The stale idea pushed by an octogenarian member (and named after them, of course) will have a tough time competing for policy support with fresh reality. The institutional powers that host cocktail parties in Washington can keep us wedded to their status quo solutions by shielding us from the real world.

On the House floor, my more industrious colleagues will approach me with their new discoveries, asking "Did you know . . . ?" Examples: *Did you know that day care costs as much as public college tuition?* (Yes, I have three kids!) *Did you know that the pandemic is prompting women to exit the workforce?* (Yes, I think about exiting every day around 7:00 P.M. when exhaustion hits me.) *Did you know that companies in bankruptcy pay bonuses to their executives?* (Yes, I taught bankruptcy law.) These members are Congress doing its best work. They have discovered a problem and are motivated to fix it.

Every student has a favorite class from school, and I have a favorite learning experience from Congress. In July 2021, in the middle of the pandemic, I traveled to the southern border between California and Mexico. Orange County is close enough to the border that fear can loom large, but far enough away that very few witness the situation firsthand. Constituents, including many immigrants, complained about border policy. They believed that migrants should follow the official process and wait in line until it is time for their lawful chance to enter our country. I stood on the famous Pedestrian West entrance at San Ysidro, the busiest land crossing in the world, and looked on both sides of the border. How long was the line? Were migrants being orderly? Were U.S. Customs and Border Patrol agents respectfully and clearly enforcing the law?

I looked in all directions. I saw fences with concertina wire, cement barricades, instruction signs, and armed guards. I did not see a line. Perhaps people were given a number and only appeared when they were called. I was there at midday, so maybe it was a lunch break. I asked immigration advocates where an asylum seeker should appear, because this was clearly not a popular location. *This is it,* they said. *Everywhere is the same.*

Later, I asked U.S. Customs and Border Protection agents to show me where screening occurs for asylum seekers. I was standing at a sign marking the entrance to the United States.

"Say I walk with my young children from Guatemala, through Mexico. I finally make it here to the point of entry. I want to ask for asylum," I asked. "Where do I go?"

They said this line was only for lawful residents of the United States.

"Where is the line for asylum seekers?" I pushed. "I am unable to return to my country and I have a well-founded, credible fear of persecution. Which U.S. government agent do I tell? Where are the forms?"

The response was silence. Under Title 42 immigration policy, a person fleeing violence could not go to our border and apply for admission. There was no lawful and orderly process because there was no process at all. If you lacked U.S. residence, you were ignored. How could migrants get in line if there is no line?

My conversations with constituents about immigration changed completely after that day. Instead of trepidation about a divisive issue, I was eager to teach people about what I'd learned at the border. From the new X-ray screening technology for vehicles to the dangers of swimming around the fence that protrudes into the Pacific, I shared what I saw. I told the stories that migrants and Border Patrol agents had told me of the dangerous and difficult situations that both groups faced. If I didn't know about an aspect of immigration, I eagerly volunteered that I'd find out. Voters sensed my comfort with the topic. That, combined with some facts and the credibility of "I saw it myself," brought the temperature down on the topic. Immigration still divides my constituents but now we are having a debate on the facts, not an argument from our emotions.

• • •

On the day in late November 2016 when I told Elizabeth Warren that I was thinking of running for Congress, she said many things. I remember only the most important thing.

"Do it. Every day in this job, you have the chance to learn something. You'll see a part of your community you never knew existed or you'll hear an argument that is totally new. Issues that you've ignored your whole life will become points of passion. You'll wake up every day with the chance to learn how to be a better American."

This is the work of Congress, and I love it.

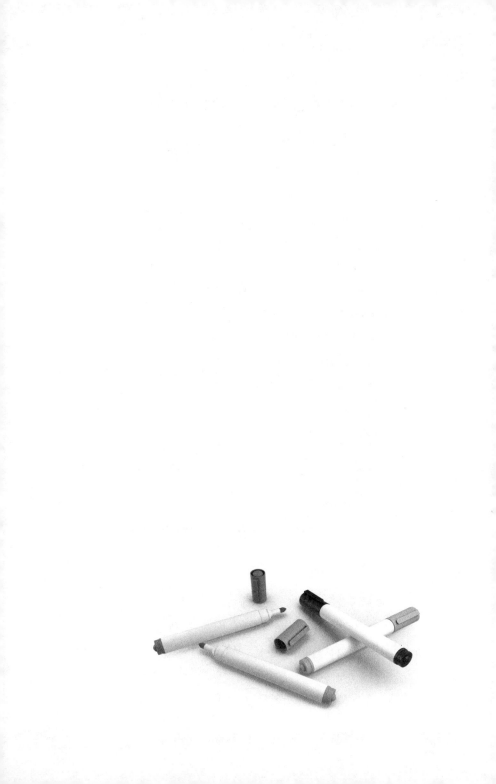

How to Contact Your Congressperson

Just ask.
Lobbyists make a living by promising to arrange meetings. Don't buy that defective product. Your quickest path to an appointment is simply using the "Request a Meeting" form on our website.

Be realistic.
Don't ask for ten minutes if you're going to get upset when the meeting doesn't last a half hour. Respect travel challenges and competing demands on our time.

Go see it.
Congressmembers are like kids; we like field trips. Invite us to tour your business, volunteer with your nonprofit, or speak at your community event.

Don't do it in D.C.
Washington, D.C., is where time goes to be wasted. To avoid missing votes in D.C., I've taken five-minute meetings squeezed into a supply closet with constituents. In our districts, meetings are longer and rarely rescheduled.

The kids are all right.
If your congressmember isn't available, ask for staff. These baby geniuses dutifully report back to representatives, whether the next step is turning your idea into legislation or avoiding you in dark alleys.

Make hard asks.
Do you want us to sponsor a bill, issue a public statement, or hold a town hall? Given that politics is often mind-bending, asking us to "keep it in mind" is a dangerously vague request.

23.

On Calculators and Cookies

Before I was even sworn into Congress, I begged Democratic leadership. I'm not proud of that, but it's true. I sent Chairwoman Maxine Waters a two-page letter, asking—really pleading—to be on the Financial Services Committee. Using an immodest phrase for a middle-aged lady, I noted that "my life's work" was studying how laws can create a stable and strong financial system. I described my oversight of mortgage companies, my advocacy to stop abusive credit card fees, my research on how families suffer when the economy struggles, and my own situation as a single parent.

Historically, members compete to get on the Financial Services Committee. Money matters a whole lot in Washington, and Wall Street has a lot of it to throw around to influence how party leaders choose committee members. Few members bring any passion for this committee's subjects: banking, insurance, real estate, housing, and securities. If those topics sound boring, you would fit right in with at least half of the committee. And if you let that boredom excuse you from gaining expertise on the issues, you would be like most of the other members. When the committee had a hearing on Wells Fargo's misdeeds, one senior congressmember explained to the bank's CEO, "Our banking system is the heart of our financial system." Um, yes. And to think that people believe congressmembers get things wrong. That statement is many things, including correct.

The Captain Obvious quality of that statement is also evidence that powerful people tend to view the economy with the same keen attention that they bring to airline safety briefings. Their plane has never crashed, so no need to listen carefully. Nearly all politicians in Washington view the economy from on high—at a distance and looking down from the top. From the vantage point of Capitol Hill, the American economy is a well-oiled machine. Government leaders just need to do regular maintenance and blame the mechanic for any breakdowns.

But up close, in the bankruptcy courts and in the days before their next paychecks, at the bottom of people's financial lives, the economy often sputters and falters. For workers laid off at age sixty, or families trying to afford housing that eats up 75 percent of their income, or former students carrying college loans for thirty years, the economy sharply defines and limits their lives. After my divorce, for example, I was grateful for the consumer protections against credit card over-the-limit fees, as childcare and alimony emptied my bank account. Four years before getting elected, I had testified before the Financial Services Committee as an academic expert about the need for those regulations to limit penalty charges. To me, the government's role in our economy is to understand why so few Americans can save anything, not just keep a steadying hand on decades-old investor protections that keep the rich getting richer.

The Financial Services Committee's job should be expanding the American dream of upward mobility. As President Trump wrapped up his first two years in office, the opposite was happening. His regulators were dismantling consumer protections and letting corporations off the hook for breaking the law. Wall Street had the advantage, and we needed to turn the tables. With sixty freshly elected Democrats in 2018, I believed my new colleagues would all see the urgency of protecting consumers and make the same committee request that I had.

Not for the first time in my early days of Congress, I was wildly wrong. Getting on the Financial Services Committee didn't require my desperate pleas to Chairwoman Waters and Speaker Pelosi. The trendy committees were Transportation and Infrastructure, Armed Services, and Small Business, all havens of easy bipartisan votes that earn no ire. Leadership was cajoling people to fill the empty Financial Services chairs, and I was easily appointed. I was ready!

But the committee was not. A couple of weeks passed, then a couple more. With a two-year term in Congress, losing a month is real time. Finally, on February 13, 2019, the House Financial Services Committee convened its first hearing of the 116th Congress. The topic was homelessness, and the witnesses were experts, just as I had been when I testified as a law professor. I asked the panel what the research showed were best practices in identifying sites for shelters and permanent supportive housing. The answer was "We aren't sure." I asked what services should be offered to help transition people out of homelessness. The answer was "We do not know a lot."

Maybe the committee just didn't have the right experts for my questions, I thought to myself. But as I listened to more of the hearing, I noticed a pattern. Democratic colleagues rambled vaguely on the topic, and then basically ended by asking, "Whaddya think?" Republican colleagues, at higher volumes, rambled on some tangential topic, like socialism (which assuredly does not cause homelessness, whatever other ills it may bring). Then they basically ended up asking, in just a snarkier tone than Democrats, "Whaddya think?"

As a professor and a parent, I know that "Whaddya think?" is an ineffective question. It might work for chatting up the person next to you at a hotel bar, but it would not get answers. Capitalism is complicated. Figuring out how our economy is doing, and who is winning and losing in its ups and downs, was going to take better questions. Or at least actual questions.

• • •

During the subprime mortgage crisis, my research had revealed how business could generate wild profits by cheating consumers. Scam artist is one of the oldest professions in the book, and even modern capitalism is premised on tough love for consumers. Buyer beware (caveat emptor, in Latin, to confuse the rest of us even more). Read the fine print. Take responsibility to protect yourself.

These principles have always been tempered with laws that require things like good faith, competition, and transparency. The idea is that people can only make good decisions to buy or borrow if they have accurate information. Back in the Stone Age, like the 1970s, when much of our modern consumer protection law was written, people did not carry around calculators like we now have on our smartphones. But still, many people today can't do math correctly, or they'll underestimate. To help, the law requires disclosures on the costs and terms of loans. Because it would be odd to disguise a law intended to make things clear, these regulations have an obvious name: Truth in Lending.

Consumers use this information to figure out whether they can afford loans. Lenders have an incentive to understate the costs of the loans they offer, as most of us will take the cheaper loan. Maybe because politicians aren't always honest themselves, Congress was clever enough to know that it would be insufficient to just require banks to be truthful. Someone would need to check the math.

The person doing that job is the head of the Consumer Financial Protection Bureau. Created after the 2009 mortgage meltdown to verify that lenders follow consumer laws, the agency addresses consumer complaints and prevents deceptive or abusive practices. In March 2019, the then director, Kathy Kraninger, came to testify before the Financial Services Committee.

I asked her to define a common lending term: "APR," or annual percentage rate. Every warm-blooded American, and even some pets, have seen this term on credit card solicitations addressed to them. When she couldn't answer, I read her the definition from the consumer-law textbook that I authored and offered to give her a copy.

Kraninger said that she had been simplifying in her response and deferred to my expertise: "A simplification I understand that you know well."

I had run for Congress when my chance to work at a financial regulator like the Consumer Financial Protection Bureau flamed out with President Trump's election. My job now was to ask the questions, not be flattered that I knew the answers. As a professor, I always knew both the questions and the answers. The point was whether the student did. Kraninger was spiraling toward an F.

I gave her the benefit of the doubt. Maybe she was not much of a wordsmith. I gave her an example of a typical payday loan: $10 charged as interest for every $100 borrowed, over a two-week loan, with a $20 signing fee. Then, I asked her to figure out the APR. My staffer handed her a calculator.

She refused to answer, telling me that the point of the hearing was to have a policy conversation, not do a math exercise. This proved my point, although Kraninger never caught on. Congress had decided it wanted the Consumer Financial Protection Bureau to check the banks' calculations, and its director could not even write down the equation.

• • •

Congress has oversight authority over the administration because if elected officials are idiots, at least the American public can vote us out (not that voters always do that; for example, Representative Matt Gaetz). Cabinet secretaries have nearly unchecked power, including the power to flounder and fail. And nobody did it better than Secretary Ben Carson. In this one regard, the man's time in government service was a shining example.

Maybe because its acronym, HUD, has an onomatopoeia problem (rhyming with "thud"), Housing and Urban Development is panned as a backwater. President Trump, following the tradition of both Democrats and Republicans, chose a human being for his administration, and then, having found nowhere else where that human could serve and not endanger our country, appointed him HUD secretary. (If you think I'm being too harsh on HUD, recall that the plot of the TV show *Designated Survivor* was that the enemy could easily topple America if the HUD secretary was the sole living successor to the presidency.)

Treasury Secretary Steven Mnuchin was set to testify the day after Secretary Ben Carson. On the plane to Washington, I waded through background readings, notes, and drafts of questions for Mnuchin. Balancing my binder on the plastic seat-back tray, I turned the page to repeat the process for Carson. But behind the Mnuchin materials was just a tab for Carson, with not even a blank sheet of paper.

A few emails later, I learned that my staff had deemed Mnuchin much more important than Carson. Nothing was ready for Carson, even though the hearing was tomorrow. The HUD secretary may be the cabinet equivalent of the last kid to be picked for dodgeball, but housing is literally shelter. Little matters more to families.

Helping people save their homes from foreclosure, I had years of experience with HUD telling me that someone would "run it up the flagpole" when I raised concerns. Now, in Congress, I could use the hearing to enlist the secretary of housing himself to address issues.

I pulled out my iPhone, found the cheery yellow Notes app, and started pecking away. The mission of FHA, the Federal Housing Administration, is to help lower-income Americans buy houses, but I knew its outcomes on the ground were less rosy. In fact, FHA was (and still is) the leading cause of blighted property in the United States. Its foreclosure policies were lousy, leaving properties sitting empty in disrepair for years.

The next day, I pulled out my questions and readied my patience. All I needed to do was ease Secretary Carson into seeing the problems. With his high-level engagement, HUD would make improvements, or, in Katie-speak, "government could fix some shit."

I asked him about how FHA punished mortgage companies for not foreclosing fast enough, rather than giving time to assist borrowers. He said he would get back to me on that.

I asked him why FHA was lousy at servicing mortgages. He would look it up and find out what was going on.

I asked him about the disparity in REO rates between FHA and other kinds of mortgages. This time there was no response.

I studied his expression, which had turned into a bit of a frown. When a student gets lost, you back up and try again.

I needed to check: "Do you know what an REO is?"

And then, Secretary Ben Carson, the man in charge of housing for our nation, asked me if I meant "Oreo."

I was talking about REO properties, bank assets called "real estate owned." He was asking me about a chocolate sandwich cookie.

"Not an Oreo, an REO." I spelled it out even more slowly. "R-E-O. Do you know what that is?"

"Real estate?" he supplied, in a hopeful voice.

"What's the O stand for?"

"Eh . . . Organization?"

"Owned. Real estate owned. That's what happens when a property goes to foreclosure; we call it an REO," I explained.

After years of studying the law and fighting for consumers, I was a member of Congress on the Financial Services Committee. And instead of getting better policies, I was tutoring a neurosurgeon.

As a professor, I couldn't expel dim-bulb students from my classes. Similarly, America was stuck with the Senate-confirmed Trump officials. I continued to explain the problem.

Secretary Carson made me an offer.

"I would be extremely happy, if you'd like, to have you work with the people who do that at HUD."

Just like with the director of the Consumer Financial Protection Bureau, the view was that his lack of knowledge was irrelevant. But as a congressmember, I'm supposed to be asking the questions, not giving the answers.

"Well, Mr. Carson, respectfully, that was my day job before I came to Congress. So now it's my job to ask *you* to work with the people at HUD."

• • •

My goal in those hearings was to show the public that Congress was doing oversight of the administration, and it worked. With the media attention, the public was getting noisy about whether President Trump's appointees were unqualified—and more important, what that meant for their lives. Take heart in this glimpse of our democracy working, if only for five minutes of questioning.

Seriously, it's important that you take heart. Because now, I'm going to tell you the worst part. These high-ranking government officials, who lack qualifications and expertise, think their jobs are jokes—like, literal jokes.

After the hearing, Director Kraninger used the hallway restroom. There, my staffer Kaylee overheard Kraninger laughing with her accompanying aide that they had bested me. Having refused to use the taxpayers' calculator to deliver answers, Kraninger pocketed it and laughed her incompetence off. In the months to come, she had the moxie to launch a major initiative to emphasize that consumers should be responsible for understanding their financial decisions.

Just a few hours after his hearing finished, Secretary Carson tweeted at me: "Oh, REO! Enjoying a few post-hearing snacks. Sending some your way." He attached a smiling picture of himself holding a package of Oreos. A couple of hours later, a family-sized box of Double Stuf Oreos arrived at my office, hand-delivered by his intern.

The fact that he sent cookies—instead of the answers I wanted—showed that for the secretary of housing, foreclosure was an opportunity to be funny and not a serious problem of people losing their homes.

The deflection from Kraninger, Carson, and other economic policy officials—Treasury Secretary Steven Mnuchin literally laughed in my face—reflects three interrelated issues. The first is straightforward. Across the board, Donald Trump put people in positions for which they were unqualified. He wasn't the first president to do that, but he certainly was the best at it.

The second problem is the false belief that our government should have no role in our economy. President Trump could appoint people without qualifications and capitalism would thrive anyway, without government. This is nonsense and wrong. A strong and stable capitalist economy needs guardrails, and it's the government's responsibility to put them in place. The pillars of capitalism—competition, access to information, enforcement of contracts, protection of private property, and consumer choice—develop from the right mix of markets and regulation.

The third issue is the most pernicious: the belief that our economy rewards the deserving (and, the unspoken counterpart, punishes those who are not). If you are making money and saving, you should be thankful to your employer and pretend the government had no role. If you are drowning in debt or struggling to put food on the table, you should remember that you are to blame and pretend the government had no role. Either way, in our economy, you get what you get and you shouldn't get upset. The government isn't responsible for your prosperity or your poverty. You are. These beliefs mask the reality that government shapes the contours of economic opportunity at every turn, from funding financial aid to allowing tax deductions on vacation homes.

Those with income and wealth sufficient to cozy up to a president and get appointed to the cabinet can literally afford to take a rosy view of capitalism and a dim view of government intervention. No experience is required for financial regulators because there is no job to do; the economy, left unchanged, continues to build their wealth. And if today's economy doesn't work for you, that's your fault.

As a law professor, I had grown frustrated with understanding economic policy but not being able to fix it. As a child of the farm crisis and a single mom worried about making ends meet, I knew the stakes for Americans. So, as a congressperson, I wasn't about to let leaders treat the government's role in our economy as a punch line. I started stocking up on whiteboards; it would take a lot of markers to expose the empty promises.

24.

Close

The pizza box lid had rings of grease from having arrived on the bottom of a tall stack of pies to the hotel ballroom last night. I flipped the lid and scanned for green. This was not a morning for vegetables or, even worse, olives. Pepperoni glistened among the hard wax of the cold cheese. I took a slice and sat down. Even in defeat, I was hungry.

"Hey, how are you?" I asked, without a trace of actual inquiry in my voice.

"Mmm," mumbled Conor, who held two slices stacked on top of each other for efficient fueling. I didn't care that I couldn't understand his answer. A big huggable guy, who worked late nights and weekends running part of our door-knocking operation, Conor usually had interesting insights about voters. This morning, however, the only person I was thinking about was myself. And yet, somehow, that required an audience, so I sat in the hotel lobby on an ivory tufted ottoman underneath a glass chandelier, while Conor munched away next to me. We looked like two college kids who had wandered into the common room after a party, scavenging because the dining hall had quit serving breakfast hours ago.

"I gotta go," said Conor, shaking crumbs off his bright orange

KATIE PORTER FOR CONGRESS T-shirt that certainly was past twenty-four hours of continuous wear. "They said to be there when it opens at nine A.M."

"Wait, where are you going?" I asked.

"The Democratic Congressional Campaign Committee in Washington, D.C., called me at five A.M. and said to get my ass to the Registrar of Voters. I was hungover from last night and I thought the pizza might help. I gotta go wake the other organizers up," said Conor. "See ya."

Conor put his duffel bag on his shoulder, scooped up a pizza box, and ambled off. He wasn't in a hurry, and I could understand why. We all just wanted it to be over. I sat there a minute or two chewing my pizza and then, like Conor, dusted myself off and headed out.

My destination was the cramped Starbucks across the street, a place attractive only to office workers escaping the fluorescent glow of cubicles. My campaign manager, Erica, had told me to meet her there, and having disappointed hundreds of thousands of people last night, I was not going to start this morning by adding Erica to the list.

• • •

Surprisingly, Election Day is not a busy day for the candidate. On November 6, 2018, my only tasks were delivering sandwiches to volunteers, greeting friends who flew in for the party, and reviewing my speeches for that night.

Polls closed at 8:00 P.M., so the party at the hotel was still gathering strength at 11:00 P.M., when Erica pulled me into a small conference room. A few staffers looked up from their computers, and the grim look on their faces made my stomach fall.

"We lost ground in the last two batches of ballots counted, and that is the wrong direction," Erica reported. "You are down by thousands. The race has not been called, though, so give Speech number three."

Speech #1 was "We won," and Speech #2 was "We lost." Speech #3, the "We don't know yet" version, signaled for everyone to go home, that the gathering was over even though it wasn't clear whether it was a celebration or a wake. While all the speeches featured a plural "we"—*we worked hard, we fought for our democracy, we know what is at stake*—I stood alone onstage, wobbling in heels. I delivered each word as written on the teleprompter, trying to convey the same optimism that had fueled our campaign against a Republican incumbent who'd won by 17 points only two years before. The audience reaction was muted, even when I pitched my voice high to signal applause. Some people hugged and cried, familiar enough with the cadence of elections to know that Speech #3 portended a loss. I'm a social crier, so I kept my poise by staring into the press cameras rather than at the crowd. Looking people in the eye and acknowledging how close we had come was just too hard.

An hour later, at midnight, I tugged a damp hotel pillow out from beneath my head. I stuffed it under the pillow beneath it, so the dry one was atop the stack. The tears kept flowing but the fresh surface was cool, like a clean dressing on a wound.

When I woke, I stuffed the Spanx, the heels, the statement necklace, and a Democrat-blue professional dress in a suitcase. I pulled on yoga pants and rode the elevator down to the lobby to meet Erica at the shitty Starbucks.

She had already dialed the first number on the spreadsheet when I arrived, and she pushed the phone across the table to me. I read from the script for every call: *Thank you so much, it was a tremendous help, I'll always be grateful, we have so much to celebrate this morning, 2018 was an amazing year for Democrats, and I'm proud to have been part of it.*

We took notes:

- LVM [left voicemail]: Linda Lipsen at American Association for Justice; Senator Kamala Harris

- MBF [mailbox full]: Adam Green at Progressive Change Campaign Committee

- SW [spoke with]: Stephanie Schriock at EMILY's List; Alicia Rockmore at DigiDems

When I dialed Ben Ray Luján, then a House member and chair of the Democratic Congressional Campaign Committee, he picked up. I started in on the script.

"Wait," he said. "I'm putting you on FaceTime."

I shot a concerned look at Erica, who looked even more panicked. My lack of care about my appearance frequently activated her sorority girl instincts, but today, even Erica had worn sweatpants and had her hair in a scrunchie.

Ben Ray's face popped onscreen, and then the camera blurred. "Hang on, I'm almost there, I have something to show you."

The camera came into focus on a hot pink Post-it note with neat script: *Katie Porter, CA-45.* It was stuck alone on a large whiteboard.

Why was he showing me this? Maybe I couldn't win an election, but come on, I knew my name and congressional district.

"Look!" Ben Ray cried out. And he moved the camera up to show a blue Post-it note that gave the heading: *Too Close to Call.*

"You're not done," he said. "You are gonna join these other folks." He panned to the left side of the whiteboard, where forty Post-it notes listed the names of flipped seats.

"We woke your organizers up and told them to get to the Registrar of Voters and observe the ballot count. It is not over yet."

When I hung up, I looked at Erica hopefully.

"That was nice of him to say," she said. And she dialed the next number. *LVM Senator Elizabeth Warren,* she noted a few minutes later.

• • •

When I arrived home at noon, some neighbor girls had left flowers picked from their yards by my front door, next to a handmade poster: WE ARE PROUD OF YOU, NO MATTER WHAT.

I tried to summon that feeling in myself, as I went inside to see my kids. I wanted to be brave and proud as the campaign that had disrupted their lives came to a close.

They wanted to know what we did now.

"Just be a family," I told them. "And clean your rooms." I started in on the mound of dishes in the sink, sweeping up the Cinnamon Toast Crunch that always seemed to spill onto the linoleum. Within a few minutes, I started to hear shouts from upstairs.

"Betsy! I told you to keep your dolls out of my room."

"It's not my fault that the garbage tipped over, Paul."

I kept cleaning, moving upstairs to the laundry: scooping single socks out of hamper bottoms, drizzling detergent on top of the pile, hefting clumps of wet clothes from the washer to the dryer. In the late afternoon, I stood upstairs and folded gray Marvel T-shirts, jewel-toned twirl skirts, and navy mesh shorts. My phone chimed alongside me. I'd been reading the messages throughout the day but had not responded. They were kind texts, sharing appreciation for the campaign and sadness about the outcome. As I reached the end of the basket, my phone started to ping rapidly. I picked up the phone, and as it kept chiming, I looked down.

5:04 p.m., November 7, 2018

63 unread messages

I clicked on the first one: "GO GIRL!"

Second one: "You love to see it."

Third one: "It's happening!!!!!!!"

Fourth one: "Please ignore my message from earlier today."

Huh.

As I stared at my phone, the display lit up with the name of my campaign consultant, Sean Clegg. On Election Day, and in the twenty-four hours since, I had heard nothing from him, Ace Smith, or the other consultants who worked on my campaign. But I'd seen the pictures of everybody celebrating at the election event for another of their clients, Gavin Newsom. As the only Democrat in a gubernatorial race in deep blue California, Gavin didn't even need three speeches. His event was sure to have more beers than tears, and I couldn't blame Sean for abandoning me to wallow in my defeat alone.

I picked up, and Sean quickly explained there was a "shit ton" of uncounted ballots, dropped off on Election Day or postmarked beforehand. Each day at 5:00 P.M., the Orange County Registrar of Voters released an updated count. Just a few minutes ago, I had closed about one-third of the gap between incumbent Republican Mimi Walters and myself.

"Close only counts in horseshoes and hand grenades," I reminded him as we hung up, and I shouted for the kids to put away the folded laundry.

During the next few days, with the late afternoon sun beaming through the west-facing windows, I folded clothes from 4:45 to 5:10 P.M. Those times are precise. I wanted to be distracted, not worried about winning or losing, as ballots posted. In those days after Election Day, I picked up not just my house but the pieces of my old life. The sacrifices of politics and service had halted. My calendar was barren, my statement necklaces were untangled from a heap in my closet, and an updated grocery list was tucked in the

As you can see, I am 100 percent dedicated to parenting.
Paul is playing video games, and Betsy is consoling herself with
a stuffed kangaroo rat that she named Peeakiss.

cup holder of the minivan. I went to the dentist and the dermatologist. I took Betsy to ballet class and packed Luke for a Scout trip to Joshua Tree. My kids were no longer "lightly supervised," as I'd joked in my campaign speeches. I was their mom, shuttling to school to pick them up, while my fellow candidates headed to Washington, D.C., for congressional orientation.

· · ·

In the early evening of the day after Election Day, Elizabeth Warren rang me. *She took her sweet time to return my call,* I thought, reminding myself that she was busy congratulating winners and had her own election victory last night. I was also being ridiculous, as fewer than twenty-four hours had passed since polls closed.

"Hi!" I chirped, determined to put on a brave face.

"Oh, Katie, I am still proud of you," she said. "You fought so hard; you really put your whole heart into it. You did a great job." She paused.

"Thank you. That means a lot," I said. "You were such a huge help."

"I loved helping you. I believe in you. Hold your head up high. I'm so, so sorry you lost."

I took a deep breath.

"Elizabeth, Elizabeth," I interrupted. "I might win." It was the first time I'd admitted the possibility.

"What?" she screeched. "What happened? My staff didn't tell me. What's going on?"

As I explained that thousands of ballots postmarked by Election Day were in the process of being counted, I heard excitement creep into my voice. I was pulling closer to victory, and there were more to count. I let myself think that maybe, just maybe, I had a chance.

With stern instructions to "keep me posted," Elizabeth hung up. Then, for the first time in months, I sat still. My imagination had gotten ahead of reality, and I started to think of what life would be like as a congressperson. If I had been elected, the laundry would be piling up, not neatly folded. I wouldn't be picking up my kids or making dinner, at least not regularly. I had no child-care provider who was willing to spend an entire week with the kids while I was taking votes and attending hearings on the other side of the country. Having spent two years unrelentingly trying to convince people to vote for me, I was again straddling the line between regular person and elected official. I wasn't sure which way to go yet.

I wondered if I would lose too much of my family life, should I win the election. I wondered why I hadn't asked myself this earlier. I realized—belatedly, to be sure—that the last real decision I'd made was to put my name on the ballot. There are no take-backs once a candidate asks the public for its trust. Many things along the campaign trail may have influenced whether I won or lost, but I had sworn an oath to the Registrar of Voters that I would serve if elected. The first step was mine, but the voters were the only ones who could reverse my course.

But in telling Elizabeth of the progress so far in closing the gap to win, I had sure sounded like someone who wanted to win. I had run for Congress to change the world—or at least some parts of it. Serving in Congress would change my life, and my kids' lives, but change was the point. Families needed affordable childcare, workers needed a bigger share of the profits from our economy, and people standing up to abuse of power in their own lives needed a government that did the same.

My phone started chiming, the message notifications coming so fast that it sounded like a steady ring. I checked my watch: 5:02 P.M. That day's ballot count must be favorable to me, I thought. Although it was unlikely that I had pulled ahead yet, I was not done with this campaign. I had relished being back in my old life, being the reassuring and present mom. But as a mom, I knew one thing for certain: The laundry can always wait.

I went downstairs, rooting around in packages of Costco toilet paper, bubble wrap and discarded boxes, and rarely worn winter coats. I emerged holding my red roller bag, the same one I had emptied when Donald Trump's election halted my plans to go to Washington in 2016. I started throwing the warmest clothes I had inside. Surely, even in mid-November, I could get away with just a short black raincoat on the East Coast. With its roomy pockets, I wouldn't even need mittens. With its hood, I could skip the umbrella, which was probably stored in my Irvine garage beside the windshield ice-scraper and sleds that I'd moved to California from Iowa.

• • •

I took a red-eye flight—with a connection, even—to arrive in Washington, D.C., on November 14, 2018, one week after Election Day. I joined the newly elected congresspeople for orientation, silently afraid my arrival would jinx the count in my race. That night, as I sat under the gilded domed ceiling of Statuary Hall, surrounded by marble sculptures of men who had shaped history, Speaker Nancy Pelosi announced that I had won the election. I barely remember that moment, but I'll never forget all the amazing, hard, fun, tough, magical, bumpy experiences that brought me to the U.S. Congress.

Elections can elate or disappoint. I've lived through both types,

Victory! November 15, 2018.

weeping with bitterness and being giddy with hope. You have too. Elections have consequences, and sometimes they are exceedingly harsh, especially on those who most need freedom, equality, and justice. But the consequences are not why elections are sacred. It's the collective and shared experiences that consecrate this democratic institution, the twining together of the rights of citizenship and the responsibility to vote that transforms regular people into elected officials. Government is full of powerful individuals, and influenced by far too many other powerful people. Elections reverse those dynamics, even in our system that has been weakened by the influence of big money, shaped by special interests, and threatened by insurrection.

The next election could be my last. Or not. The decision is yours. And mine. Either way, I'll have laundry piles to tame, family and friends to enjoy, and a country to serve. The same is true for you, and I'm damn grateful for that.

Acknowledgments

Luke, Paul, and Betsy Hoffman, my children, deserve credit that this book isn't any more cringe or sus than it had to be for the sake of truthfulness. Their honest feedback is burned in my soul: "This book reminds me why I don't read autobiographies." I appreciate your tolerating leftovers for dinners and unsupervised early mornings as I carved out time for this project. And thank you for agreeing to the publication of this book, after "considering your rights."

In the challenging, exhilarating months at the end of my first campaign and the start of my service in Congress, Julian Willis saw the potential of this book. Turbulence and time never shook his confidence in my abilities as an author.

I'm sure there's a better way to say this, but Jordan Wong, you are the best book bitch a girl ever had. Thank you for being my constant companion during this process. I appreciate your rule number 1, but Nora Walsh-DeVries, I need to say thank you for making it possible for me to be a congressmember, candidate, mother, and author—all at the same time.

Frank Spring gave me a framework for storytelling and invaluable feedback on ideas and structure. Lara Horgan provided a quiet space for winter writing. Katie Bartizal, Nathan Click, Katharine Meyer, Maximillian Potter, Lynh Tran, and Michael Troncoso read chapters or drafts, providing just the right mix of encouragement and critique. Michael Pratt and Jordan Wood were early enthusiasts for this book, as were Julia Cheiffetz and Rakia Clark. Rich Davis solved my subtitle problem with creativity and generosity.

My agent, Carolyn Savarese, understood me and my voice, advocated for this project, and gave me invaluable guidance from the first outline to publication day. Don't lose my number; I have more books in me! Plus, I want to be your friend forever. The Crown team, especially my editor, Libby Burton, kept this book on track; my copy editor, Lawrence Krauser, helped this know-it-all really know it all about grammar.

I thank my teachers and professors of writing: Kathryn Dudley, Andrea Heiss, Lois Rose, Jean Sheridan, Liz Porter, and those who improved my writing as frequent co-authors of past books and articles: Pamela Foohey, Sara Sternberg Greene, Bob Lawless, John Pottow, Tara Twomey, Deborah Thorne, Elizabeth Warren, and Jay Westbrook.

My friends Karen Cohn, Anthony and Mimi Falcone, Masu Haque-Khan, Dara Sorkin Michelson, Mallory Rome, Vicky Schulte, and Angee Kerrigan Simmons kept me smiling and laughing through the difficult moments. Finally, thank you to my parents and siblings, especially my sister, Emily Porter, who was the first person who let me lead.

Art Credits

About the Author

Katie Porter represents Orange County, California, in Congress. Prior to being elected in 2018, she was a law professor and consumer finance expert. Porter lives with her three school-aged kids in Irvine, California.

katieporter.com
Twitter: @katieporteroc